From the Heart
of a Servant

From the Heart of a Servant
Poetry Created to Glorify God

C. R. Lord

Tate Publishing & *Enterprises*

From the Heart of A Servant
Copyright © 2007 by C. R. Lord. All rights reserved.

This title is also available as a Tate Out Loud product. Visit www.tatepublishing.com for more information.

No part of this publication may be reproduced, stored in a retrieval system or transmitted in any way by any means, electronic, mechanical, photocopy, recording or otherwise without the prior permission of the author except as provided by USA copyright law.

Scripture quotations marked "KJV" are taken from the Holy Bible, King James Version, Cambridge, 1769. Used by permission. All rights reserved.

The opinions expressed by the author are not necessarily those of Tate Publishing, LLC.

Published by Tate Publishing & Enterprises, LLC
127 E. Trade Center Terrace | Mustang, Oklahoma 73064 USA
1.888.361.9473 | www.tatepublishing.com

Tate Publishing is committed to excellence in the publishing industry. The company reflects the philosophy established by the founders, based on Psalm 68:11,
"The Lord gave the word and great was the company of those who published it."

Book design copyright © 2007 by Tate Publishing, LLC. All rights reserved.
Cover design by Kellie Southerland
Interior design by Lynly D. Taylor

Published in the United States of America

ISBN: 978-1-60247-762-9
1. Non-Fiction, Christian   2. Poetry

07.09.27

Dedication

This manuscript is dedicated with immense gratitude to
My Lord and Savior Jesus Christ
who alone has delivered me from sin,
death and eternal misery!

It is also dedicated to my wonderful lifetime
companion who shines bright before the Lord and
humanity as a tremendous example of what a wife
and mother should be. Beverly Ann—God's greatest
gift to me apart from His wonderful salvation!

Further this manuscript is dedicated to my exceptionally
special children who have loved me enough to put
up with all my whims and shortcomings in raising
them! To Samuel, Christopher, Richard, Kristine,
Abigail, David and Sarah. Seven very special
gifts bestowed by a loving Heavenly Father!

Finally, this manuscript is dedicated to anyone
who has influenced my life in any manner whether
it was negative or positive because every precious
experience contributed to my growth and character
building, and helped make me a better man.

To all the above I say, Thank You from
the innermost depths of my being!

C. R. Lord

September 10, 2007

Table of Contents

Foreword 11
Preface 13
My Testimony 15
Introduction 23
   Praise 23

Jesus and God 25

   I've Got Jesus 25
   Two Kings 26
   Jesus 27
   Jesus Is 28
   Jesus Loves Me 29
   Marvelous, Wonderful, Holy God 30
   Oh God, How I Wonder 31
   O' Mighty God 32

The Body Of Christ 35

   Costly Doctrinal Foolishness 35
   Hear O' Church 37
   Lopsided Preaching 39
   O Give Me A Church 41
   Pray On Christians, Pray On 42
   The Key 43

Babies and Children 45

   A Little Child Looked Up One Day 45
   It's A Privilege 47

Me and My Cat and My Little Bear	49
My Mean Parents	50
Our Children/God's Gifts	52
Wee Little Hands	55

The Things of Life — 57

Be Encouraged	57
Despair	58
How Can I Forgive?	59
In A Rush	62
Like Children	64
My Flesh, My Enemy	65
This House	66
Woman	68

Epic Poetry — 69

Christianity	69
Count the Cost	74
Freedom In America	78
Genesis One	82
Is There A Devil?	84
Jonah, A Whale Of A Tale	87
The Proud Cloud	90
The Year Poem	92

Miscellaneous Poetry — 97

I Set My Face	97
My Surrender	99
Rebellion	100
Sleep	101
Couplets	102

A Song Poem	103
Books	104
Long Before the Sun Rises	106
Our World	107
Poetry	108
Praise Him	109
Reflection On Easter	111
To A Sweet German-Italian	112
Try To Imagine	114
Lord, Please Help the Other Man	116
Dusty and Jann	118

Non-Poetic Writings   119

Introduction	119
A Day Without Doors	121
A Word To Those Who Call Themselves Christians	123
Hear O' Church	123
Child Of Darkness Or Light?	131
I Find Myself Laughing	134
The Secular Media and Christianity	137
Reflections On Important Matters	140
Leadership	144
Management	145
The Man Who Would Please Everyone	146
Baby Congratulations	149
Rick's Pawn Shop	150

Some Closing Thoughts   151

Foreword

Once you begin reading this book by C. R. Lord, you will be convinced, as I have been, that he is an apt man of letters, an agile poet and a creative and gifted writer.

Because books are unique presents, windows into the heart of the author and excursions for readers' imaginations, you will have a blessed and challenging journey through Rick's expressions and vivid word pictures.

I have known Rick and his dear wife, Bev, for almost thirty years. As alumni of the school co-founded by the Reverend David Wilkerson and me, I know and appreciate their strong desire to share the reality of Christ with others. Their investments in the lives of their own seven children prove their faith and reveal the fruit of their pursuit of God.

Hang on for an emotional, mental and spiritual challenge to your life as you open up your heart to the inspiration in the pages of this book. You will be blessed.

Dr. John Q. Kenzy

President of the Youth Challenge
International Bible Institute

Sunbury, PA

Preface

The poems and other writing in this book came into being over a period of time from February 19, 1974 to the present day. They were written in a wide variety of places under various circumstances, and a number of them were born through the personal life and ministerial experiences of the author.

Poems like "It's A Privilege," "Wee Little Hands" and "My Mean Parents" were born from experience as a parent raising seven children. Other poems such as "I Set My Face," "My Surrender," and "O God How I Wonder" were based on experiences in the author's personal life and ministry. Furthermore, there are a variety of poems covering everything from a poem about poetry, to a shocking poem about rebellion and its possible consequences. Undoubtedly, there is a poem in this volume that will relate to everyone who reads it.

The few Non-Poetic writings are entertaining ideas, such as "Rick's Pawn Shop." Two very important articles that are challenging messages to Christians and non-Christians alike are: "Whose Child Are You," and "Reflections On Important Matters."

It is not the author's intent to be merely entertaining, but to produce a work that will minister to others. It is the author's earnest hope that what is presented here will draw others closer to God—challenging, comforting, exhorting, and in every way possible helping people appreciate life more and love God with all their heart!

We have a short span of time on this planet, and we must

learn to invest that time wisely for ourselves and all we come in contact with in our sphere of life.

If this book does any or all of the things it sets out to accomplish, it will be well worth the time invested in producing it for those who meditate on its contents.

My Testimony

Simply put, I once was blind but now I see! After years of living in a party lifestyle using alcohol and drugs, God reached down to me and totally revamped my life. Later, He gave me a wonderful family, and has given them all the gift of eternal life through His Son and the boldness to testify of their faith without fear to any that will listen.

Since then, He has added to our family, a daughter-in-law and a son-in-law. Both know Him and serve Him. In addition, we are into our sixth month of being new grandparents to a very sweet and well-mannered little girl named Keira. My wife and I have been greatly blessed to have one another, and have children that will remain faithful to our Lord Jesus forever. We are very thankful and give all praise, honor and glory to Jesus who alone is worthy!

I was born on September 27, 1942 at about 1:00 am during a strong rainstorm. I was married on January 7, 1979 during a day filled with rain, snow, sleet and hail. I asked the Lord that when I leave this earth to be with Him—it be a bright, shiny day on earth—just as it will be for me in His presence and as it was when I first came to know Him! How wonderfully radiant and glorious it will be to enter His presence forever!

I have no memory of my life from birth to eight years old. When I was eight, my father decided he would get rid of me and my older brother, who was born crippled. He took us, without my mother's knowledge, from Pennsylvania to Michigan. There he left us with a family that we had never met, and he never returned. That family had no desire to keep us and treated us very badly. Shortly thereafter, I was taken by another family in Michigan and separated from my brother.

My mom found my brother soon after, and he was able to get home. It took a year for my mother to find me, but that year was pleasant to me because the people were kind and wanted to raise me as if I was their own son. There is so much that could be said about this one year, but suffice to say, it was my first introduction to God—as the people who had me for that year were very dear and loving Catholics. I always thought it was special that their last name was *Good*. It was through this incident that I began to hate my father, and that hatred lasted for twenty-three years.

When I was eleven years old, my mother was trying desperately to work and take care of five children at the same time. Frustrated, and with remorse, she was forced to place three of us in an orphanage. The orphanage was in Lewisburg, Pennsylvania, and was also a farm, so I enjoyed time to get in the fields and work. I didn't care for the staff, which at times were kind, but at other times, very cruel; however, the farm and the other children made life there bearable.

I met my very first girlfriend at that place, and just like my wife, her name was Beverly. To put all speculation to rest, they are not the same person.

An event took place during that time that is marked in my memory forever. There was one staff member, an old, white-haired lady, who would gather us around her knees at night and talk to us kindly and tell us stories. One particular night, she told us that she had a dream the previous night. What she told us I have never forgotten. She told us she was in Heaven, walking about in a dazzling white robe and she saw a lake that she immediately jumped into and began to swim. In a short while, she climbed out and her robe was immediately dry. That evening, she went to be with her Lord. What a wonderful way to pass into His presence! This incident was my second contact with someone sharing something about God.

My mother remarried when I was sixteen, and we were brought back home from the orphanage. I am sure beyond any doubt that my stepfather had no idea what it would be like to have five of us, plus one of his own at home, and he didn't know how to handle it. Soon, he was drinking, and one time he was hitting my mother, so he was arrested and she divorced him. There is so much more than that to tell, but for the sake of brevity, I will close this chapter of my life with my graduating from high school and going into the United States Air Force at the age of seventeen.

An item of great importance is that at the age sixteen I attended a church near our home and went forward to accept Christ as my Savior. I am sad to say that I wasn't taught that there was a Christian life to be lived on the other side of salvation that would involve commitment and daily struggles. Because my salvation had very little substance and no power to live victoriously, I fell.

The Air Force was more demanding in those days than it is now. Discipline was strong, and I resented it. As a result, my time was spent foolishly. At the tender age of nineteen, my party life started. I never really wanted to drink alcohol, but a broken romance pushed me over the edge. I centered my life around a beautiful girl, and she left me to marry someone else without telling me. Later, after writing a number of letters, her mother, out of sympathy for me, wrote and told me she was married. I was so crushed that I stayed in a drunken condition for over four months. This led to twelve years of alcohol use, which included six years in the drug culture. The years I wasted in this lifestyle could fill a book, so I will mention a few significant events that greatly influenced my life during those years.

I met Kay somewhere between a marijuana joint and a beer... or was it a snort of speed? My memory of this is non-existent. We ran the streets, partied and "fell" in love; we were married within fourteen days of meeting one another. After I married her, I learned about her schizophrenic problems, which included infidelity, suicidal tendencies, her on-again-off-again love for me, and finally, a trip to a mental institution.

Her parents and siblings hid that from me; or, perhaps they did try to tell me but I was too drugged up to listen. The last thing I remember of her before my conversion to Christ was visiting her in the mental institution. She greeted me warmly and said she was glad to see me, and then turned on me and said she wanted to kill me.

My irrational rationalizing solidly convinced me that Pennsylvania was my real problem, so two friends and I hopped into a van with a pound of marijuana and headed for Fort Lauderdale, Florida for fun-in-the-sun, girls, dope, booze and parties. Shortly after, I was arrested while my friends were somewhere calling relatives in Pennsylvania for money to help us get back. It was a strange experience because I had never been arrested and it seemed surreal—kind of like an Al Capone movie but happening to me. So my friends' high-tailed out of there with promises to send some aid back to me. Those promises of help never came, or came after I was released and they had no way of contacting me.

Eighteen days later, I was released from Broward County Prison and set out to find God. You see, until my arrest, I had been too busy to see that I was wasting my life and had no purpose or direction. I am sure beyond all doubt that being arrested was the final step to my being arrested by the Holy Spirit so I could finally find this tremendous peace that comes from knowing Christ as my Savior and God as my Heavenly Father. It was in prison that I cried out to God saying, "If you are real and can prove it to me—I will give you my life." Needless to say, He did, and He did it in such a way that there will never be any doubt that He did it. Nothing anyone could ever say or do could convince me otherwise.

So much has transpired since that time that it would be difficult to relate in detail, however some of the highlights of significance are included in the next paragraph.

My first year and one month as a new Christian were busy with street evangelism, ministry in front of bars, prostitution districts, and other sordid places, as well as beaches in Florida and California. As a matter of fact, I was saved one night and put on a street corner the very next morning and told to witness. God worked a miracle in me reaching back fifteen years into my memory and giving me verses to answer questions I couldn't have answered otherwise. Because of this experience, I will not accept the excuses people in churches give for not taking the gospel to the lost. If God cannot empower you, He is not big enough to serve—He isn't interested in our ability as much as He is in our availability! God graciously gave me bold and fearless leaders who taught me to live for others and to sacrifice so that others could come to the saving knowledge of Jesus Christ. When I left that ministry I was able to minister on the streets of my hometown by myself, which eventually led me to Bible college, my very special wife, seven children, and ten years of ministry to people who came from the street as I had. This foolish man, who was never stable in anything and who couldn't be faithful to a job or anything else for over a year at a time, has radically changed. My walk with God is thirty-three years on February 19, 2007. My marriage has lasted over twenty-eight years, and I have been able to be a Father to seven children for almost twenty-six years. I have faith that these things will continue until I go home to be with my Lord forever, in spite of my many shortcomings. It is God alone who is faithful to keep us in all things.

Somewhere in that period of time, I began to write poetry and then various articles. I prayed and asked the Lord for a pen name that would glorify Him and point to Him. He gave me one that I am solidly convinced could come from Him and Him alone—C. R. Lord—"See Our Lord." I believe this is our purpose in life—that others may not see us, but by His matchless grace, they will see Him reflected in our lives so they too may come to know Him.

I am now burdened with the shallowness that is clearly evident in the lives of many who call themselves Christian in this generation. A multitude of people we know and love are lost and dying without hope, while the body of Christ has become soft, far too comfortable, and desensitized to much that would have made Jesus cry out from a heart pierced with sorrow. Things that would have shocked God's people years ago have become commonplace to us; so many of us have no deep, compelling burden for the honor of our Lord and for the salvation of those who are lost. Travail and anguish that God's name is mocked, God's people are mocked and the world is lost and dying without hope has died out among us.

I believe it is in God's heart to see revival come to this generation; not the revival that is a man-made scheduled event with time constraints, but strong and convincing moves of the Spirit of God. I believe that revival will only come in response to Christians crying out with weeping and deep travail of soul. It will begin with sorrow for our own sloth and indifference, and deep desire for renewed vision and purpose, and then deep yearnings that many may be delivered from darkness at any cost through our lives. It will culminate in sacrificial living that others may be delivered from spiritual destitution, ignorance and blindness before it is eternally too late for them. It will be Christ-centered and glorify God, and will be abasing to man because we will seek to honor God and God alone! The world will see and wonder, and the tide of evil will be turned for a time before the end comes.

Joel speaks that during the last days, there will be a great move of the Holy Spirit. Oh, how we need to get ready to be vessels that God can use to pour out his mercy on this wicked and perverse nation! It is well past the time that those who call themselves Christian should rise from their slumber, shake off the shackles that bind us, and move in the power and anointing of God so He will not be ashamed of us when He returns.

Consider this... if God can turn a foolish and hell-bound sinner like me from darkness to light, using him to reach others, then He can also turn many others in the same way if the people of God will repent and do what He has called us to do. What if those who call themselves Christians would put aside all their excuses and fears of man and seek God for power that fulfills His purpose? What if those Christians would go out into the highways and byways searching for people just like me who are bound by drugs, alcohol, lust and many other things? We, through the power of the Holy Spirit, could turn this world upside down for Christ! Will we?

C. R. Lord

Introduction

This little poem expresses my motivation in presenting these gifts from God, to you, the reader. To Him alone be all honor, glory, and praise!

Praise

>Should praise be given for a gift,
>That God alone can give?
>Yes, but to God be all the praise,
>As long as we shall live,
>
>For He is worthy of our praise,
>Our God, and Him alone.
>So friend, direct your praise to Him,
>For of it I'll have none.
>
>He made my mind and heart to see,
>When they were blind by sin.
>He gave the love that teaches me
>To have deep peace within,
>
>So, if what's written here can bless
>Your life when things look dim.
>Just lift a thankful heart above
>And give the praise to Him.
>
>*C. R. Lord*

Jesus and God

I've Got Jesus

I've got Jesus in the heart of me,
And if you want to see,
You'll have to take a look into my eyes and see,
The joy He placed within,
When He took away my sin from me.

C. R. Lord

(A Child's Song—for big and small children)

Two Kings

I love to write about my King.
His name is dear to me.
He cleansed me of my many sins,
And set my spirit free.

I used to serve another king,
Of dark and fearful mien,
But since I've met the King of kings,
I'll not serve him again.

Oh friend, the Prince of Darkness grim,
Would damn your very soul.
But Jesus Christ the Prince of Peace,
Will cleanse and make you whole.

What folly then to serve a king,
Of lesser pedigree,
Repent of all your sin right now,
My King will set you free.

C. R. Lord

Jesus

February 6, 1986

Justice demanded death for sinful man,
Judgment was sure so God devised a plan,
Joyous the news rang out for all to hear,
Jesus has come, fear not, be of good cheer.

Eagerly shepherds ran to seek this child,
Entering in they saw Him meek and mild,
Excellent glory they began to tell,
Everywhere speaking of Emanuel.

Shepherds in joy returning to their sheep,
Sweet baby Jesus quietly asleep,
Shining angelic choirs tell of God's love,
Stars burning brightly in the sky above.

Unworthy man has since that day received,
Untold rich blessings when they truly believed,
Unctionized truth about the blessed One,
Unmeasured love displayed in God's own Son.

Shout! So the entire world may hear and see,
Salvation offered—blessed, full and free,
So many walk in darkness yet today,
Show them the Savior ere they pass away.

C. R. Lord

Jesus Is

Jesus is the sweetest word to fall upon my ear.
The sunshine living in me that is brighter every year.
The strength I need to carry every burden that I feel.
Reality within a world where very little's real.

Jesus is a name as soft as velvet summer breeze.
A whisper of ecstatic prayer when I am on my knees,
A total new experience of heart and soul and mind,
The treasure I am sorry that it took so long to find.

Jesus is the answer when I'm lying sick in bed.
Or when the devil finds a space and creeps inside my head,
Always strong and never failing when we call His name,
From the very dawn of time He's always been the same.

Jesus means to never fear whatever trial may come.
The power to cast out the spirits of the deaf and dumb,
And charge all demons to depart from every human living,
He shows the beauty we can know when we begin forgiving.

Jesus more than anything has borne our grief and shame.
Humiliated, scorned, and beaten when we were to blame,
We never could deserve that gift received from God above,
The blood of Jesus shed for us, the perfect gift of love.

Jesus breathe it, pray it, say it, o'er and o'er again.
Master, Savior, King of kings, and yet He calls us friend,
Greater love has never been nor evermore will be,
And we've been blessed to live with
Him throughout eternity.

C. R. Lord

Jesus Loves Me

OCTOBER 9, 2004

In a little town where I was born,
A song was often heard,
Many a lovely Sunday morn,
Before they preached the Word.

A simple song of love and grace,
That everyone could sing,
That told of Jesus in the place,
We came to meet our King.

The words rang out from young and old,
We put on quite a show,
With voices ringing strong and bold,
He loves me—this I know.

For centuries the hardest men,
Who stopped to listen in,
Believed those precious words again,
Delivering them from sin.

Yes, Jesus loves me, this I know,
So simple and so true,
It's real within my heart, and so,
I offer it to you.

C. R. Lord

Marvelous, Wonderful, Holy God

Marvelous, Wonderful, Holy God,
We lift our hearts in praise,
Astounded at your matchless care,
Toward us all our days,

Awesome, Magnificent, Lovely God,
Your beauty lies within,
The multitudes your Son has touched
And freed from death and sin.

Omnipotent, Omniscient God,
The earth proclaims your power,
With every passing sunset,
And each refreshing shower.

Terrible, Vengeful, Angry God,
The wicked shake and fear,
Knowing that your judgment falls,
On those who will not hear.

Oh the sadness my heart feels,
For those who spurn your grace,
Glorying in sin and shame,
And will not seek your face.

C. R. Lord

Oh God, How I Wonder

Oh God, how I wonder,
In my mortal frame,
How one so unworthy
May mention your name.

Oh God, how I wonder,
At mercy divine.
That touched on a soul
As wretched as mine,

Oh God, how I wonder,
In worship and praise,
At perfect forgiveness,
For my wicked ways,

And still more I wonder
At my wicked heart,
Which seems so reluctant
In doing its part.

Oh help me my Father,
To give back that love.
You've poured out so freely
From heaven above,

Then use me Lord daily,
That love to proclaim.
That others might wonder
And honor Thy name.

C. R. Lord

O' Mighty God

O' Mighty God from age to age,
Eternally the same,
In vain the heathen 'gainst Thee rage,
And curse Thy Holy Name

My soul within is pierced with woe,
And sorrows as I see,
The multitudes who will not go,
To meet my Lord with me.

The power of the devil's hold,
On lost and wretched men,
Through alcohol or lust or gold,
Shows me the strength of sin.

I walk the streets and knock on doors,
And much to my chagrin,
These same poor souls profess to me,
"I once was born again."

O' God I cry, how can it be,
That some who know your name,
Can live in such hypocrisy,
And show no sign of shame?

O' Jesus, Jesus, help me please,
To never love you less,
And keep me Lord upon my knees,
And teach me righteousness.

What horrid thought to turn away,
From you who loved so well,
And suffered cruelly on that day,
To save our souls from Hell,

Oh, help me turn some back again,
Salvation to renew,
And let me touch some poor lost men,
That they might turn to you.

Then one sweet, glorious day we'll sing,
Together 'round the throne,
Hosannas to our God and King,
For praise is His alone.

With multitudes our voices raise,
As Heaven joins and sings,
Eternal melodies of praise,
To the great King of Kings.

C. R. Lord

The Body Of Christ

Costly Doctrinal Foolishness

Oh, how we strive and battle so,
As verse by verse we cite,
God's word with great intensity,
To prove our view is right.

Baptidzo means immerse some say,
No sprinkling must be true.
Foot washing must be done,
Or I'll not fellowship with you.

Baptism in the spirit with,
The gifts is real my friend.
If you don't have all nine,
You don't make heaven in the end.

Now as for those who speak in tongues,
Emotional! Oh my!
If they should come to my home church,
I surely think I'd die.

Praise God, I'm Pentecostal,
I cannot understand.
How all those fundamentalists,
Would dare to take their stand.

So, on we go in foolishness,
In bigotry and pride.
With "love" toward the brethren,
If they'll kindly stay outside.

And not attend "our" fellowship,
Corrupting "our" belief.
And all the while our Savior weeps
In unrelenting grief.

"Put off your foolish strivings,"
He cries out from His throne.
While you continue in your sin,
The devil's left alone.

To drag souls screaming into hell
Every single hour.
Forget your proud obnoxious views,
And seek my face for power.

Oh, look beyond these petty things,
Seek peace and love "all" men.
Reach out and touch the millions who,
Are dying in their sin.

If all of you will do this work,
And nurture it with prayer.
All differences will be erased,
And you will find me there.

C. R. Lord

Hear O' Church

February 5, 1984

Oh the wondrous love of Jesus when he came to save!
Oh the mystery of His glorious victory o'er the grave!
Oh the awesome weight we carry who would do His will!
Oh the sinful hearts that hear Him and reject Him still!

As we hear His awful warning to a sinful race;
Can we sleep while men are dying at an awful pace?
Can we rest while souls are feeding on the husks of life?
Can we see the millions lost and stay back from the strife?

Now the Master sends a call to those who bear His name.
Will we listen and obey, or hang our heads in shame?
When the roll is called up yonder, will we meet someone?
Who, through our response to Him,
has come to know God's Son?

Brethren, let us rise above the little things that keep
Us from running to the battle, for our Lord's lost sheep.
Let's go on nor fear of dying keep us from the strife.
Snatching many from Hell's fires to eternal life.

Let us fight with banners flying, every evil foe;
Shouting victory, striking boldly, never letting go.
Striking out with strong assurance in that blessed one,
Who will bring us to the kingdom with a sweet "Well done!"

Was a higher call e'er given? I must answer, "No!"
Do we wish to fail Him now, who has loved us so?
Oh, eternal matchless glory! How can we delay?
Let us give our all for Jesus; let's begin today!

C. R. Lord

Lopsided Preaching

A lopsided gospel is preached today,
In pulpits across the land,
Misrepresentation and disarray,
Are found on every hand.

The worldly and carnal find phony peace,
As lopsided preaching persists,
The talk of God's love puts the sinner at ease,
In the church of the Liberalist.

But lopsided preaching is also found,
In searing descriptions of Hell,
As many who live in sin are told,
God condemns every infidel.

And men live in comfort or fear of Him,
Who reigns in the heavens above,
The Ruler whose justice is not a whim,
But perfect as is His love.

What damage this lopsided preaching has done,
Only God in His wisdom can know,
But it's sure to continue unless we shun,
All this vain and pompous show.

Our preaching must hold the whole counsel of God,
Not only a part of the whole,
God's justice and love are sufficient to prod,
The blinded and sin-laden soul.

Why should we withhold one jot of His Word,
From multitudes blinded by sin,
The lopsided preaching that many have heard,
Has kept them from entering in.

To the truth of the gospel and Christ's saving power,
That sets every willing one free,
Repent of this foolishness this very hour,
And set them at liberty.

If such words offend you then preacher beware,
Your words may condemn you one day,
Our Lord is demanding and He will not spare,
The servant that will not obey.

C. R. Lord

O Give Me A Church

(Sung to the tune of "O, Give Me A Home.")

O give me a church where the dead in Christ roam,
Where the saints are all busy at play,
Where naught will disturb, no exhorting is heard,
And the people have not learned to pray.

O give me a church where the preaching is sweet,
Where picnics and banquets abound,
Where folks smile and sing of the Savior and King,
And challenging words are not found.

O give me that church and I'll die in my sins,
For it's sure that nobody will tell,
That I ought to obey Christ who is the True Way,
Or I'll find myself lost and in Hell.

Chorus

There Christ is not known,
And the preaching is dry as a bone,
And the devil with glee laughs at their poverty,
While the world in despair dies alone.

C. R. Lord

Pray On Christians, Pray On

People dying all around us,
Ruined with sins awful blight,
Are there any intercessors,
Yielded to the Spirit's might?

O' how desperate is the need!
Never was the world so vile.

Countries warring constantly,
Harlots roam with luring smile,
Recreation is our theme song.
Immortality runs wild.
Sports arenas draw the crowds.
Terror stalks the little child.
Is there any intercessor,
Aching for the world's relief?
Never was a need more pressing,
Seldom has there been more grief.

Pleading from His throne in glory,
Reaching out to you and me,
Ah we have to listen for our,
Yieldedness will set men free.

On, with tears and groans, the world,
Needs them O' so desperately!

C. R. Lord

The Key

In our records of revivals,
There's a truth we all must see.
There can be no true revival,
When the church neglects the key.

We have tried so many methods.
We give seminars galore.
We think God must surely honor,
What He surely must abhor.

For our crusades and our seminars,
Without his holy fire,
Must fall far short for certain,
Of His innermost desire,

All our guesswork and presumption,
Fail to gain the slightest praise,
From the God of all creation,
Who has numbered all our days.

What he really seeks within us,
Is submission to His will.
And we'll never know what that is,
If we can't learn to be still,

For the key the church is missing,
Won't be found by anxious care.
The true secret of revival,
Is believing, earnest prayer,

We can learn to hear God speaking,
If we'll bow on bended knee,
And we'll see a great revival,
When we learn to use the key.

C. R. Lord

Babies and Children

A Little Child Looked Up One Day

MARCH 9, 2000—1:57 P.M. EST

A little child looked up one day,
Never heard that she should pray.
-But-
When she saw the heavens above,
Was struck with wonder at God's love.
A man came by and saw her look,
Had in his hand a little book.
- And-
Began to tell her of God's grace,
And Jesus met her in that place.
How sad men struggle all alone,
As God calls to them from his throne.
-Just-
To offer love from day to day,
If they will bow to Him and pray.
How strange a little girl can see,
How Christ has come to set men free.
-When-
Men full grown go on their way,
And never think to kneel and pray.
Well, God is merciful and wise,
He wants to open paradise
-So-

If you hear his call of love,
Just raise your heart to him above.
Then like the little girl you'll see,
The only one who sets men free.
-He-
Who died to save the human race,
From death and Hell and sin's disgrace.

C. R. Lord

It's A Privilege

December 30, 1985

It's a privilege,
As you watch a baby come.
In the operating room,
From a pregnant mother's womb,
What a privilege!

It's a privilege,
When you hear that newborn cry.
And from deep within you sigh.
And you sense your wife's reply.
Wondrous privilege!

It's a privilege,
As you hold within your arms,
All those lovely little charms,
And you still those first alarms.
Precious privilege!

It's a privilege,
When you take the child with you,
As he makes his first debut,
And the compliments ensue.
Special Privilege!

It's a privilege,
As you dedicate this one,
To God's Only Blessed Son,
And the work is thus begun.
Glorious privilege!

Let's not minimize one jot,
The importance of this tot,
Let us give the best we've got,
It's our privilege!

C. R. Lord

Me and My Cat and My Little Bear

10/18/2004

Me and my cat and my little bear,
Are kneeling for a bedtime prayer,
We're asking Jesus through His might,
To keep us safely through the night.

We ask for angels to come down,
Protecting everyone in town,
We pray that Dad and Mommy too,
Get peaceful sleep the whole night through.

We ask the Lord in Heaven above,
To touch my brother with his love,
And give him dreams that will be sweet,
And brand new stockings for his feet.

Then with a heart filled full of joy,
And hope that nothing could destroy,
We thank Him for the blood He shed,
And quietly we go to bed.

C. R. Lord

My Mean Parents

My mom and dad are very mean.
I'd like to trade them in.
It seems no matter what I do
It's classified as sin.

I only want to stay up late,
And let my homework go.
Well, anyway, it could be done,
After I watch this show!

And surely meat and vegetables,
Can't be as good as pie,
And soda chips and pretzels,
And candy, My oh My!

These things provide the energy,
I need to run and play.
It gets exasperating,
When I cannot get my way!

But wait, here in the Bible,
I see God's holy plan.
Children obey your parents,
If you'd grow to be a man.

Believe God gives them wisdom,
To raise you for His glory,
Then with them in eternity,
You'll tell a different story.

With praises to the Lord of Lords,
Whose blood has made you clean,
You'll see my friend that after all,
Your parents weren't so mean.

C. R. Lord

Our Children/God's Gifts

October 27, 1999

Softly the prayer began,
  Awesome God send us a man.
    Make him to know and love your Son,
      Until a thorough work is done.
        Enlighen him so all will see,
          Love flow through him unceasingly.

Christ we beseech Thee now,
  Help this boy to learn,
    Righteousness full and free,
      Incline his heart to burn,
        So he may serve with grace,
          Touching the lives of those,
            Only in purity and love,
              Patient with power from above,
                Holding the lonely close.
                  Echo yourself through Chris.
                    Righteous Lord please do this.

Reach down and calm this heart.
  Inspire him with your peace.
    Chasten this boy continually.
      Help all his strivings cease.
        Almighty, loving King,
          Roll waves of love o'er him.
            Direct his soul to sing.

C.R. Lord

Kind and merciful God,
   Reach deep and draw her out.
      Ignite a fire within her soul,
         So she will want to shout.
            Triumph despite her Lord,
               In love reach down and make,
                  New and full impressions, and
                     Empower her for your sake.

Almighty, Father God,
   Before your Holy Throne,
      Infill her with your Spirit Lord,
         Give grace and joy within,
            Ability to love all men,
               Increasing sense of you, and
               Loving kindness too.

Dig deep inside this heart,
   Allow your power to fill,
      Vindicate and purify,
         Inspire, empower to testify,
            Devoted to your will.

Softly seal your word,
   Affix it deep inside,
      Refine this heart,
         And fill with you,
            Holy Ghost abide.

We offer Lord these gifts You sent,
    Entrusting us to raise,
        Each one with only one intent,
            That they might learn your ways.

Accept them now we pray,
    And hold them in your care,
        That we might all one day,
            Be reunited there.

Wee Little Hands

December 30, 1985

Wee little hands that are squeezing my face,
    Make my heart feel strangely warm.
And in that soft, chubby childlike embrace,
    There's no intention to harm.

Wee little hands reaching out for a hug,
    Wanting relief from distress.
After a fall on the living room rug,
    Close to your bosom they press.

Wee little hands feeling fragile and small,
    Wearing a bruise or a scar.
Picked up when brushing a nail in the hall,
    Show just how needed we are.

Wee little hands buried deep in a bowl,
    Covered with noodles and cheese.
Unfettered by care, absorbed in the whole,
    Testing each bite with a squeeze.

Wee little hands all too soon will grow old,
    Soon may lose life's fleeting breath.
Oh, let us love them before they lay cold,
    In the unchanging stillness of death.

C. R. Lord

The Things of Life

Be Encouraged

March 25, 1986 - 8:30–8:45 a.m.

Be encouraged, for the storms of life will pass.
It is well known that the dark night leads to day,
And life's raging seas with calm as clear as glass,
Will reflect the brilliant sun's sweet healing ray.

God intended that the trials of life should come
To enrich us with the lessons we must learn
To prepare us for our great eternal home
At our Lovely Lord and Savior's sure return.

Be encouraged then in this life's little while
Heaven gazes down upon us through it all
And the saints who passed before with knowing smile
In excitement, with us, wait the trumpet's call.

Rather labor through your sorrows filled with praise
For exceeding joy that nevermore will cease
Is complete in Him who measures all our days
Who alone gives life and joy and strength and peace?

Despair

Standing on a corner near a trash can at the square,
Knowing God is with me, and yet feeling He's not there.
Seeking for a sign from Him to loose this devil's hold,
Wanting to be in the Spirit where I can be bold.

Silent with this burden having prayed for his relief,
To break the power of Satan, and this unrelenting grief,
Waiting for his answer so my spirit will be free,
To share the message of his love for us on Calvary,

I feel so vague and empty when my spirit's turned away,
So tired and void of feeling in a deathly sort of way,
O' Lord, please come and save me in my hour of despair,
I need you more than ever Lord to answer this one prayer.

C. R. Lord

How Can I Forgive?

How can I forgive?
The thought tormented me.
How can I erase
This haunting memory,

Seems I just relive,
The way that I was used,
And I can't forget,
How I was abused.

My mind like a film,
Keeps playing o'er and o'er,
All the wrongs and hurts,
Done to me before.

Will there be no end,
To this deep, painful state,
The more I dwell in this,
The deeper grows my hate!

Suddenly a knock,
Disturbs my angry thought.
A minister of God stands there,
And suddenly I'm caught,

My mind goes back to days,
I went to Sunday school,
And in the presence of this man,
I feel I am a fool.

My memory races back,
And dimly I recall,
Something I heard of as a child,
Of One who died for all.

I asked him to sit down,
He opened up God's book,
And after years of my neglect,
I finally took a look.

As God's man shared with me,
God's wondrous grace to man,
I bowed my head in deep remorse,
And my tears freely ran.

I felt His cleansing power,
Flow mightily through me,
And in the presence of God's love,
My anger had to flee.

Oh, sweet forgiveness from above,
The hatred I had felt,
Seemed so unclean, unholy, and
My heart began to melt.

The Spirit of the Living God,
Compelled me to forgive,
And as the weight was lifted,
I finally could live,

And peace, sweet peace filled all my thoughts,
New life was born that hour,
Forgiveness is no problem now,
For resurrection power,

Has lifted me above myself.
My heart has been made new.
Oh friend, submit to Christ today.
He'll do the same for you.

He'll free you from the suffering,
That unforgiveness brings,
And fill your heart and mind each day,
With precious, holy things.

C. R. Lord

In A Rush

I look around this world we're in,
See folks rush here and there.
And wonder why they don't slow down,
Perhaps they wouldn't dare.

So many deadlines must be met,
We scurry to and fro.
Perplexed, distressed, just worried sick,
'bout what we do not know.

We'll miss the train, the bus, the plane,
Oh hurry, don't be late.
We rarely think to plan ahead,
We're in an awful state.

Appointments press upon our minds,
The dentist's chair at two.
Then school to get the kids, then home,
Oh, what are we to do?

The supper must be done by five,
When Dad comes home to eat.
Oh hurry up, we must get dressed,
We have our friends to meet.

Rushing here and rushing there,
We ramble on and on.
Impatiently, we fret and stew,
Our sanity is gone.

My friend, God never meant for us
To fuss and worry so.
But look to Him and calmly trust,
He'll keep us as we go.

If we'll just listen to His voice,
He'll make His purpose clear.
There'll be no need for us to rush
As we serve Him down here.

C. R. Lord

Like Children

How dear and precious is a child to me,
A lesson for this oft' proud heart to learn,
Of beauty that is simple—trusting—free,
O'er which a multitude of people yearn.

We wish for just an hour we could regain,
The wonder and the joy that childhood knows,
Forgetting all our failure and the pain,
Yet, in our hearts a frosty coldness grows.

And all the years we never can recall,
Are felt with deep remorse, and in regret,
We sit and stare so blankly at the wall,
And somehow feel there must be some hope yet.

Then from the shadows of our life we hear,
A message clear and simple to our mind,
Of childlike faith in Him who is so dear,
Who died a cruel death for all mankind.

With tears we come before Him soiled with sin,
And know the cleansing touch He died to give,
As youth eternal bubbles up within,
From death we rise and really start to live.

Oh, let us ever be like children here,
And putting off our foolish prideful ways,
Keep minds and hearts and spirits free and clear,
To love and serve the Master all our days.

C. R. Lord

My Flesh, My Enemy

My flesh, my enemy—vexation of my soul,
The author of accursed lust, that keeps me from my goal.
Of unretarded service to the God I long to serve,
Who pulled me from the destiny of Hell that I deserve.

My flesh, my enemy—a cross so hard to bear,
I know I'd serve Him fully if it only wasn't there.
My spirit hates with perfect hate, the enemy within,
The old man seeking deathly hard to pull me into sin.

My flesh, my enemy—it sometimes hurts so much,
I lose the faith to even claim my Master's healing touch.
I seem so far away from him—so up against his will,
I lose all peace and get confused until He makes me still.

My flesh, my enemy—my trial and my shame,
It seems I never will be clean to call upon his name.
An even though I know He's gonna cleanse me by and by,
I know my flesh, My enemy is with me 'til I die.

C. R. Lord

This House

This house is always open,
But thieves had best beware.
Because this house is guarded,
By constant daily prayer,

We offer you our bathroom,
To shave and clean up in,
But, don't take nothin' from this house,
'Cause stealing is a sin.

The food is to be eaten,
Don't overstuff yourself.
And when you've washed your dishes,
Return them to the shelf.

The washer's in the cellar,
With lot's of soap inside.
So, wash your clothes and dry 'em out,
But please don't swipe our Tide.

Relax and read our Bible,
And if you'd like to stay,
We'll welcome you when we get back,
And all of us can pray.

For God gave us this blessing,
To share with everyone,
This house to lead all hungry souls
To His redeeming Son,

And when we enter Heaven,
A new home waits us there.
Prepared for us by God Himself,
Who taught us how to share.

C. R. Lord

Woman

Woman was a gift from you,
When you created earth.
Taken from the rib of man,
'Twas you who gave her birth.

Beautiful above all things
In Adam's paradise,
A help for him from you O' God,
From you who are all wise.

And when she led him into sin,
By eating from the tree.
You blessed her Lord despite herself
And her iniquity,

You gave her sons to till the fields
And daughters for her own,
You blessed her seed through all of time,
Despite the way they've grown.

You blessed a woman with your Son,
She suffered when He died.
And when He rose up from the grave,
Her soul was purified.

C. R. Lord

Epic Poetry

Christianity

November 15, 1977—1:35 a.m.

For thirty-one years I couldn't see
The truth of Christianity
Because my sin had kept me blind
It really never crossed my mind.

A list of sins could only show
How very little I did know,
About the Christ of Calvary,
Who gave His life to set me free.

But, Praise His Name, my vision cleared,
And in Him I no longer feared,
The dread unknown that gave me fright,
Before he made my darkness light.

At first I was so overjoyed,
That every sense was there employed,
In awestruck wonder at the change,
My Lord had seen fit to arrange.

Expressionless, I could not find,
The words to share my state of mind,
So clean, so sure of peace at last;
It happened O' so very fast.

I wanted all the world to see
The Christ who made the change in me.
I knew that I would just explode,
If everybody wasn't told.

The days and weeks and months went on,
And not an ounce of zeal seemed gone,
But slowly I was brought to see
Some very harsh reality.

Not everyone was overjoyed
And many really got annoyed,
When I stood up with radiant grin
And told how He had cleansed my sin.

They cursed and mocked His Holy Name,
And some would even put the blame
On God for all their misery.
They too were blind and couldn't see.

How sad, I thought, to watch them die.
My burdened heart began to sigh,
And cry to God to understand
The power of sin on every man.

And then, amazed, I felt the pain,
As truth struck deeply once again,
And I saw sin in Christians too;
The ones who had been born anew,

"Why aren't they perfect?" my heart cried;
These ones for whom my Savior died,
How can they care so little for,
The Lord they all claim to adore?

My pride had blinded me so much;
I evidently had lost touch
With simple truth—we were yet men,
And sinful yet—though born again.

Praise God for men who had prevailed,
And lived to tell me how they failed,
And then forgiven fell again;
Yet God had cleansed from every sin.

Who took the time to clarify
That our sin nature didn't die,
And that much struggle would ensue
Before this earthly life was through.

In love, they showed my pride to me.
Praise God for their sweet honesty
Against which I rebelled those years,
And wept so many needless tears.

Praise God, Praise God, O' Bless His Name!
For those whose life has but one aim;
To build true soldiers of the King,
And gladly give up everything,

Who count all things but dung to win
This precious Lord who frees from sin,
And only long that others too,
Might come to love Him as they do.

How wonderful! I've been set free
Again as when he first touched me
And now I have begun to see
Small bits of Christianity.

I see the need for change each day
For all who walk this narrow way,
And how we're fooled so easily
By what we think, and what we see.

In multitudes of thought and word
One message clearly can be heard;
"Surrender all—surrender all!"
Hold nothing back for he does call,

For full control in everything
As Master, Savior, Lord, and King,
For He alone can mold and bend
Our Christian lives for us, my friend.

There is a certain way to grow,
And many things that we can know
For God's own word will make them clear
To all of those who wish to hear.

Just read and pray and fellowship,
And let the Spirit get a grip
Upon your thoughts and on your heart
Beseech Him never to depart.

Become a witness every day
In everything you do and say.
Avoid such things as cause you strife,
And seek to live a Christ-like life.

Let none persuade you from His way
No matter what they do or say,
For fiery graves do surely wait
All who let Satan seal their fate,

Temptations, trials—whatever be;
Cling to our Lord tenaciously,
Stand firm! Keep drawing ever near
Until your life is finished here,

And when you reach His rest at last,
And all tumultuous times are past;
You'll gaze at Him and clearly see
The truth of Christianity.

C. R. Lord

Count the Cost

Revised 1988

The Savior calls us unto Him,
And shows us lives a-burning dim,
Then asks, "Will you go speak my name,
To pull these from eternal flame?"

We quickly answer, "Yes, we'll go,
To Heaven above or Hell below,
Yes, anywhere to reach the lost,"
But some forget to count the cost.

The cost is prayer and deep travail,
It's fasting often to prevail,
Its burdens for the souls of men,
Which breaks our heart in grievous pain.

The brokenness that burdens bring,
The promised times of suffering,
The fierce attacks of evil powers,
At all the inconvenient hours,

The cost is willingness to spend,
Long days and nights up with a friend,
Reach out to those in prisons too,
And love all those who spurn our view.

If we persist in serving well,
We will incur the wrath of Hell,
And every scheme will be applied,
To see that victory is denied.

A preacher, brother, sister, friend,
Will all conspire to bring our end,
Policemen, lawyers, judges too,
May hinder us in what we do.

And after all of these have failed,
When Satan sees that we've prevailed,
He'll seek with a malicious grin,
Some other way to do us in.

Remember Jesus and be strong,
Deny the liar and sing the song,
Of Him who called each one who's lost,
And also had to count the cost.

Our Lord gave far beyond the price,
Of anything we'll sacrifice,
He left a kingdom and a throne,
To make us His and His alone,

He suffered curses, spit and shame,
That we might have life through His name,
The thorns and nails and cross he bore,
To make the world's salvation sure,

The wicked passed to mock and sneer,
A soldier pierced Him with a spear,
And in a moment dark and grim,
The Father turned away from Him.

We say we'll miss the games, the fun,
Our joy should be in Christ the Son,
Must we give up the things we own,
Did not our Lord give up His throne?

Our jobs and time and family,
To open eyes that cannot see,
Well what will people think of me?
Who cares, it's Christ that they must see.

The Savior calls once more O' man,
And shows to us His master plan,
"Who'll go? He cries as once before,
Behold, I'm standing at the door."

Then quietly some walk away,
But some determined they would stay,
And be sent forth whate'er the cost,
By Him who died to save the lost.

What will we do as Jesus cries,
"Look on the fields! Lift up your eyes!?"
The value we place on a soul,
Will turn us from or toward our goal.

Let's count the cost before we start,
Search every corner of our heart,
No price we pay could be too great,
To save a sinner from his fate,

Oh listen to the Savior's call,
As it goes out to one and all,
His heart is breaking o'er the lost,
Let's answer, "We will pay the cost."

C. R. Lord

Freedom In America

We have freedom in America
At least that's what we're told
Yet many are impoverished
While others hoard their gold.

We are quick to point the finger
After all, they have the chance
To engage in private enterprise
And improve their circumstance.

It is obvious they are lazy
Living off the tax of those
Who work hard and lengthy hours,
To provide their food and clothes,

We debunk and downgrade others
Cast aspersions on their name
Though we never talked to them about
The reason for their shame,

We have freedom in America
It's abounding everywhere
Evolution can be taught as fact
While we ban all classroom prayer.

We have laws protecting eagles
While a million babes are slain
Women's rights must be protected
Slaughtered infants can't complain.

In our "wisdumb" we have risen
And proclaimed ourselves to be
Wiser than the Master Planner
Who fills all eternity.

Hardly caring that He watches
Every hour of the day
We had better put our foolishness
Aside and learn to pray.

We have freedom in America
For the great majority
But we've ignored the little groups
That fought for liberty.

The inventors, mocked and scorned, stood firm
We reap from all their toil.
Small farmers feed the teeming mass
From their labor in the soil,

Men and women battled slavery
At the loss of life and limb
Pioneers traversed this country
And their vision would not dim.

Small businesses whose smiling clerks
Had willing hands and heart
Gave meaning to free enterprise
They played a major part.

But now the little man is set
Conveniently aside
Swallowed up and all but lost
In the overwhelming tide

Of industry and larger farms
And corporate dynasty
We travel this destructive road
Leaving trails of misery.

We have freedom in America
But Oh the cost is great
The family—our nation's strength
Disintegrates with hate.

Our youth hang out on city streets
And no one seems to care
There is little love in homes and schools
They must find love somewhere.

Pornography spreads like a plague
Sex crimes are getting bolder
They're practiced on the helpless child
All the while our hearts grow colder,

Corruption in our government
Is found at every level
So many thinking they are wise
Are blinded by the devil.

So on and on the list could go
The rapes, the killing sprees
The suicides, the child abuse
The endless miseries.

Like the deluge in Noah's day
Sin inundates the land
And though the Word of God is heard
Men "will not" understand.

We'd best wake up and see our plight
Before it is too late
Our freedom will become the chain
That seals our mortal fate.

This nation then will cringe in dread
As they are made to see
True freedom only comes through Christ
And lasting liberty.

But at that time 'twill be too late
The Judge of earth and Heaven
Will seal this country's awful fate
And justice will be given.

C. R. Lord

(REVISED 1988)

Genesis One

In the beginning God
First words in Genesis
Created Heaven and earth
A perfect work was this.

"Let there be light," He said,
And darkness fled away.
So God created day and night
And that was the first day.

Then on the second day
The waters did divide
God made the firmament above
And oceans deep and wide.

The dry land next appeared
At our Great God's command
Then grass and trees and lovely flowers
That third day filled the land.

The fourth day sun and moon
And stars in bright array
Were set in Heaven by our God
To light the night and day

The waters teemed with fish
And music filled the air
As birds sang out on the fifth day
A swelling, grateful prayer.

The sixth day He made beasts
According to His plan
Then crowned His great creation
And made a perfect man.

Then, from the man, a woman
And everything was blessed
And finally a seventh day
Was set aside for rest.

For years these things remain
No season in remiss
Thus showing clearly God's great power
In one of Genesis

My friend, do you know Him
Without whom none can live
Who breath and health and strength and life
To every man doth give?

If not, seek Him today
He holds so much in store
For those who love Him he bestows
True joy forevermore.

His peace will fill you here
And far beyond all this
For He alone deserves your trust
The God of Genesis.

C. R. Lord

Is There A Devil?

Is there a devil? Would you kindly tell?
Is he the ruler of a place called Hell?
Does he have legions at his beck and call?
Is it his highest joy to see men fall?

Is there a devil? I would like to know.
Dwelling in blazing depths of fire below?
Does he devise and scheme from day to day
Devious plans to lead blind men astray?

Is there a devil? Atheists answer no.
They theorize that it just can't be so.
Why should they let the devil myth persist
When the informed know God does not exist?

Is there a devil who is in control
Of the unwary, lost and simple soul
Wielding his power o'er the helpless clod
Who's never found the strength that comes from God?

Is there a devil? Theologians cite
God's Holy Word, the Bible must be right.
God never lies, His word is true and pure
There is a devil; that we know for sure.

Is there a devil? Controversies rage
As every man proclaims himself a sage,
But these conflicting views can't all be true.
What's an unlearned and ignorant man to do?

Is there a devil? We had best find out
Ask God to show us and erase all doubt
If he is real and we die in his spell
We will awake to find ourselves in Hell.

Is there a devil? I believe my friend
If we deny it or choose to pretend
He can't exist, our death will make it clear
There is a devil in this earthly sphere.

There is a devil who is filled with hate
Dangling before us his infernal bait
Endlessly tempting ever to conspire
To drag us screaming to eternal fire.

There we would see him vile and filled with dread
As judgment falls upon his rebel head
With him to live in unrelenting grief
With him in torment never find relief.

We ought to listen to God's Holy Word
Receive the message we've so often heard
There is a devil, but do not despair
Christ will defeat him; come to Him in prayer.

Give Him your heart and soul, your strength and mind.
He is the Lord and Master of mankind
He'll give you victory o'er the devil's power
And keep you safely hour after hour.

All through your life the battle will not cease.
Satan will tempt you, Christ will give you peace.
Then on the day you draw your final breath
You'll be victorious over Hell and death.

Satan, in rage, must watch you as you rise
To meet the Master far beyond the skies.
Oh friend believe the devil does exist
Don't listen to the foolish atheist.

The theologians message is from God.
Follow it closely as you walk this sod,
Or you will die beneath the devil's spell
Doomed to eternal life with him in Hell.

C. R. Lord

Jonah, A Whale Of A Tale

I want to tell you a whale of a tale
'Bout Jonah, a prophet of God
Who jumped on a boat and then set sail
Away from the path he had trod

It seems God had a task to be done
So he called on Jonah to do it
Of course we know with God on his side
There would have been nothin' to it

But Jonah, a disobedient son
Rebelled at this special calling
And foolishly turned from God on the run
The beginning of every man's falling

His prejudice caused a blindness to come
To his heart which had grown quite cold
The hardness within didn't leave any room
For any but Jews in the fold

Well, he jumped on a ship, but he quite forgot
That God always sees everything
And sooner or later, like it or not
He was going to serve his King

The Lord of Hosts sent a violent storm
That set Jonah's boat to shaking
And while Jonah slept below in the warm
The crew on the deck was quaking

It didn't take long for them to see
That Jonah was causing their trouble
So Jonah told them, "Cast me into the sea
And do it on the double."

Down into the deep old Jonah did sink
But God, in His love, had a plan
A fish swallowed Jonah while taking a drink
To preserve God's rebellious man

He spent three days and nights in a jail
No man would think to fashion
He had plenty of time to weep and wail
O'er the foolishness of his passion

Then he called out to God and repented
Of his bitterness, hatred, and pride
And the Ruler of Heaven relented
When He heard how old Jonah cried

He caused that whale to spit Jonah out
Then put him back on his mission
But amazing enough, we hear Jonah pout
'Cause he secretly had been wishin'

God would change His mind and destroy those men
After all, they wouldn't repent
But to Jonah's surprise they heard and obeyed
The word Jonah's God had sent

Now Jonah was angry and told God so
He didn't want them to live
But God clearly let His prophet know
That he needed to learn to forgive

All men are of infinite value to me
I love them and they need to know
If any will turn from iniquity
Then I will most surely bestow

Abundant grace and pardon free
And receive them as my own
To live in love and joy with me
In worship 'round My throne.

C. R. Lord

The Proud Cloud

(For my children—January 4, 1987)

Long ago and high up in the sky,
Yet easily in view of human eye,
Lived a large and fluffy cloud of gray,
Who was making rain both night and day.

He was very good at making rain,
But he drove the other clouds insane,
For though they worked as hard to rain as he,
He thought his rain the best that there could be.

And every chance he had he let them hear,
About the storms he made both far and near,
He told them how he made the rivers rise,
And how he blotted sunlight from the skies.

He told them how he touched the fields of flowers,
And helped them live and grow by his great showers,
And while the stories he would tell were true,
He did no more than other rain clouds do.

The other clouds grew weary, as would we,
Of list'ning to his boastful vanity,
And so they held a meeting to decide,
What they could do to end his awful pride.

They all agreed that they would need to ask,
The Lord of all to undertake the task,
For He alone would know just how to make,
This foolish rain cloud see his great mistake.

The Lord God listened to the rain cloud's plea,
Then gave an order from eternity,
At once a mighty wind blew from above,
And broke the cloud in pieces, for God's love,

Knew what was best to help him understand,
That all his rain had come from God's own hand,
That if it weren't for God who reigns on high,
He couldn't send one raindrop from the sky.

I hope this story brings a message plain,
So every time we watch the clouds and rain,
We will recall that God in His great love,
Has poured out all our talents from above.

If we use them in doing something great,
That causes many folks to celebrate,
Then lift our hearts in pride from day to day,
God's love could take our talents all away.

The rain cloud learned a lesson we must know,
If we would live as we should here below,
The message most important in this story,
Is that God alone is worthy of all glory.

C. R. Lord

The Year Poem

Just as each new year begins
   All of life must have its start
      Nothing comes but by design
         Unto us from God's great heart
           Almighty wisdom gives
              Resisting, mankind grieves
              Yielding, mankind lives

From Pisgah's lofty height
   Each part of life we'll see
      Becomes a small part of the whole
         Reflecting on the human soul
           Uncluttered by our fears
              Above the clouds of doubt
                 Redeeming grace will clear our view
                    Yielding peace the whole year through

Meanwhile some choose to stay
   Among the clouds of gray
      Reality is lost
         Christ's precious love is tossed
         Heinously away

Amazing grace still cries
   Please listen to my plea
      Repent of all your wickedness
         Incline your ear to me
           Listen and be set free

Multitudes today
  Are lost and gone astray
    Yet still refuse to pray

Jesus God's own Son
  Unto His own does cry
    Now's the time to wake O' church
      Ere many more should die

Judgment follows death
  Undying souls must know
    Leave all your hindrances behind for
      You are called to go,

And warn the fools and slow
  Unwilling to believe
    God's word is sure
      Unchanging and it's
        Satan would deceive
          Then mock them as they grieve

Salvation has been sent to
  Everyone who'll trust the Lord
    Prostitutes and drunkards, all who
      Trusting in God's word
        Elect to live and serve him
          Mourning every sinful way
            Boldly standing for the right
              Ever forward in the fight
                Resting in the Savior day by day

Oh the Glory of it all
   Can our finite minds contain
      Total freedom from the law of sin
         Our hope with Christ to reign?
           But how many never hear
              Eternal love so dear
                 Reaching out with power to loosen every chain

Now's the time while it is day
   Oh dear Christian join the fray
      Very soon we'll hear the trumpet, and
         Eternity begins
           Many souls in many places
              Beg to see our cheerful faces
                 Exhorting them to turn to Him who
                    Rescues men from sin

Don't delay or give excuses
   Every day there's more abuses
      Christ is seeking to commission
         Erstwhile men who will obey
           Multitudes today are crying
              Broken, hurting, lost, and dying
                 Every effort must be made to
                    Reach them ere they pass away

C.R. Lord

(*Alternate*)
Don't delay or give excuses
  Every day there's more abuses
    Can't you hear the cry of
      Evil men all looking for a door?
        Many children now are weeping
          Bound to realize the reaping
            Evermore to be tormented
              Roasting in Hell's awful roar

C. R. Lord

Miscellaneous Poetry

I Set My Face

1987

I set my face to do God's will
And bravely started out
Determined that I would fulfill
My pledge and never doubt

I ran against the gates of Hell
Flags flying, sword aflame
Eager to face each obstacle
In Jesus' Holy Name

The difficulties barred my way
Yet I, undaunted fought
Dethroning self and yielding all
At least that's what I thought

But fierce, relentless conflict soon
Left me somewhat distressed
As pressure from the foe increased
And greatly 'gainst me pressed

"This is too much," I cried aloud
For God to ask of man.
And looking for a place to rest
I turned my back and ran

The Lord in mercy carried me
Off the field of war
And set me down to rest and learn
And help me to mature

You ran into the battle son
Before you could prepare
What you must learn I'll teach you
If you'll come to me in prayer

You were impetuous and young
In spirit matters new
Before I send you out to fight
I'll make a man of you

And for what seemed eternity
The Lord put me aside
And dealt with motives, attitudes
Ability and pride

He taught me that my confidence
Must be in Him alone
And many lessons I must learn
Before His work is done

Now I have set my face again
And I confess with joy
A confidence that rests n Him
Which nothing will destroy.

C. R. Lord

My Surrender

It is not my surrender Lord,
I know within my heart.
There is no willingness to give,
Even the smallest part.

I have no care for holy things,
Dear self I must preserve.
I only want the best for me,
More than I could deserve

Surrender? Oh my flesh cries out,
You ask too much of me.
Won't you accept a certain part,
I cry out desperately.

Surrender all the spirit calls,
I can't my soul replies.
And shrinking from my cross I see,
Grief in my Savior's eyes.

I can't. This time with tears I fall,
Hard at the Master's feet.
"Then give me your weakness, He replied,
I'll make your surrender sweet.

Then light poured upon me from His face,
His truth filled my heart with peace.
As He took my weak and wavering will,
Surrender was sweet release.

C. R. Lord

Rebellion

While sitting in my room one day,
I took time to reflect.
Upon the straight and narrow way,
Set here for God's elect.

It seemed constricting to my view.
The cost was in excess.
But my close study of God's word,
Showed he would take no less.

Indignantly I paced the room,
Determined to find how,
To circumvent the will of God,
My soul refused to bow.

I stormed outside and down the street,
Defiance in my face.
If God won't bend then He can get
Someone to take my place.

Engrossed in rage with rebel heart,
I never heard the yell.
That warned of my impending doom,
'Til I woke up in hell.

C. R. Lord

Sleep

October 24, 1976

An awesome foe I warrant thee.
A foe that many never see.
Who creeps up softly to your bed,
And bids you linger 'til your dead.

Some welcome him with no alarm,
Because he seems to bring no harm.
But God's Word warns, "Beware lest he,
Should bring your soul to poverty."

Proverbs 6:10–11, 20:13, 24:30–34

C. R. Lord

Couplets

> Fall upon your knees and pray,
> Lord what should I do today?
> If you listen you will hear,
> His instructions, loud and clear.

> The Son is shining through my day,
> As I am traveling on my way.
> And every hour is filled with light,
> As I make him my first delight.

C. R. Lord

A Song Poem

"I Was Sinking Deep In sin,"
In a deep quagmire.
When "Amazing Grace" reached down,
And snatched me from the fire.

It was "The Love of God" for me,
That kept me all the years.
And finally brought me "Near The Cross,"
And banished all my fears.

I heard "There's Power In The Blood,"
To wash our sins away,
And felt the "Springs of Living Water,"
Flow through me that day.

Now "Come Ye Thankful People Come,"
I sing so all will hear.
"Look to the Lamb of God" and live,
He's always very near.

"Rejoice and Sing," "He lives" I cry,
To every listening heart,
"Trust and Obey" this precious Lord,
And ne'er from Him depart.

C. R. Lord

Books

The world abounds with many books
Of varied shape and size
With multitudes of topics from
Both foolish men and wise.

This is to be determined by
The reader as he looks
Superficially or deeply at
The content of the books.

There are books that cover everything
'Bout fixing boats and cars,
Books concerning methods known
For making fine cigars.

Books that teach us etiquette,
And show us where to eat,
Books to teach us canning,
Or the cutting up of meat.

Books of crossword puzzles,
Books of mystery,
Books that teach us how to sew,
And books of history.

Books by great philosophers,
Books by jokesters too,
Books discussing anything
You want to know or do.

With all this book variety
It's difficult to know
Just what to read or to believe
Or on which path to go.

And so to leave confusion
From all of these behind
I sought and found the noblest
Of writings I could find.

I opened up the Bible
And as I knelt to pray
The Christ who is the "Living Word"
Cleared all the mess away.

C. R. Lord

Long Before the Sun Rises

10/27/2004

Long before the sun rises, while some are sleeping hard,
The hunter quietly steps outside heading for the yard,
The winter was severe this year so deer group tight together,
Seeking food beneath the snow in very chilly weather.

Oh God, the hunter prays, give me success this day,
Help my aim to be precise and painless to the prey,
And then he trudges on in snow up to his knees,
Feeling numbness in his hands from the morning breeze.

Suddenly a light shines through breaking up the night,
Oh Lord, he sighs, you're wonderful—
you fill me with delight.
The brilliant orange and yellow rays bouncing off the snow,
Remind him of his Lord's redeeming touch of long ago.

Recalling all the hunting trips in drunken wasted days,
His heart is filled with gratitude, his
mouth is filled with praise.
He senses God's sweet presence and lifts a smiling face,
To thank Him for His bounteous love,
His mercy and His grace.

C. R. Lord

Our World

    Our world—created from chaotic mass
    Concealed in darkness, open to our God
    Devoid of life as we know life to be
Where foot of man, nor beast had ever trod.

    Our world—but for our God's creative power
    Would lie unfruitful, cold and fully dead
    But in God's word the story is revealed
That God brought light and life and love instead.

    Our souls—chaotic bound in vilest sin
    Enclosed in darkness, known to God alone
    Dwelling in death, yet feeling so alive
Without the blood of Christ which can atone.

    Our souls—but for our God's redeeming grace
    Doomed to torments, nevermore to cease
    The "Living Word" comes to our hearts revealing
    The way to pardon, life and joy and peace.

C. R. Lord

Poetry

Poetry says many things
Some of them very true
But poetry could n'eer express
The love God has for you.

The words existing in the world
Inadequately say
How faithfully He guides our feet
Along the narrow way.

Nor could our meager words express
His patience when we fail
Or how His mercy picks us up
And helps us to prevail.

What words pray tell, could be brought forth
Sufficient to declare
His Father's love that knows and feels
His children's every care.

So speech must always stand amazed
Confounded and undone
For finite words can ill describe
The One who gave His Son.

But how resplendent will we sing
With words no more our own
In heavenly language to our King
Forever 'round His throne.

C. R. Lord

Praise Him

March 15, 1984

Praise him in the sunshine.
Praise him in the snow.
Praise him when it's seventy,
Or, when it's ten below.

Praise him in the morning.
Praise him in the night.
Praise him when you're sorrowing,
Or, bubbling with delight.

Praise him during sickness.
Praise him in your health.
Praise him in your poverty.
Praise him for your wealth.

Praise Him for a baby girl,
Or, for a baby boy.
Praise Him for that special mate
Who fills your heart with joy.

Praise Him for the food you eat.
Praise Him for your drink.
Praise Him for the mind which has
Enabled you to think.

Praise Him for your hands and feet,
And a voice to sing,
Wonderful sweet praises to
Our glorious Lord and King.

Praise Him that you're free from sin
Let praise fill all your ways.
For every good and perfect gift,
Offer up your praise.

And as death draws you nearer
In your life's final days;
Look back upon his bounteous love
And give the Lord more praise.

Then entering into Heaven
A lovely anthem raise.
Before the Lord of glory
Sing endless songs of praise.

C. R. Lord

Reflection On Easter

On Easter day men gather
For festive celebration,
In almost every place we know,
Throughout God's vast creation,

Some dress in fancy clothing,
They wear one day a year,
Some gobble Easter candy,
While others guzzle beer.

Bright colored eggs are hunted
Every Easter day,
And so to all appearances,
Things seem bright and gay.

But oh, how grieved the Lord is,
And how His heart is broken,
For men in all their foolishness,
Have missed the words He's spoken.

This day was meant to honor Christ,
Who died and rose again,
A bruised and bleeding sacrifice,
For vile and sinful men.

C. R. Lord

To A Sweet German-Italian

(Written for my wife in Bible College)

I like-a you face,
I like-a you hair,
I like-a to take you,
Everywhere.

I like-a you nose,
I like-a you lips,
I like-a you soft,
Little fingertips.

I like-a you ears,
I like-a you cookin',
I like-a how you are,
So very good lookin'.

I like-a you legs,
I like-a you feet,
I like-a you ways,
So gentle and sweet.

I like-a you more,
As each day comes and goes,
From the top of you head,
To the tips of you toes.

I like-a so much,
What you say and you do,
But what I like-a most,
Is the Jesus in you!

C. R. Lord

Try To Imagine

> February 5, 1986

Try to imagine, if you can, how sweet
It was when Mary knelt at Jesus' feet
While quietly she listened to Him tell
The things that made her very being swell.

What precious words upon her ears did fall
What priceless moments as she centered all
Her powers to listen as the Master spoke
What sweet emotions o'er her spirit broke.

Try to imagine Martha rushing 'round
Her busy feet just barely touching ground
Trying so hard her blessing to prepare
Unwittingly allured by Satan's snare.

Of busyness, no time to hear her King
So overwrought 'bout every little thing
Stopping to murmur to the Lord and then
Rushing right off "her work" to do again.

Oh Martha, Martha can you hear Him say
So many things disturb your peace today
Yet Mary's found what will not fade away
Follow her lead, be still my child and pray.

Well might we all this lesson come to know
As in our day we scurry to and fro
Like Mary see the one thing needful now
And quietly before our Savior bow.

C. R. Lord

Luke 10:38–42

Lord, Please Help the Other Man

(A silly song that teaches a valuable lesson on pride)

Verse 1

Today I had a problem, and I didn't know what to do
And so dear Lord I've come tonight to ask advice of you,
You see there is this brother; I'm sure that you know who,
It seems he'll never listen when I "Tell" him what to do,

Chorus

So Lord please help the other man—I know he's not like me,
'Cause Lord you know I'm always
kind and sweet as I can be,
And Lord I'm always trying to lend a helping hand,
So Lord won't you please talk to him,
and help him understand?

Verse 2

Now Lord I know I should've prayed
for him a whole lot more,
'Cause Lord there's beauty in his life,
I know you could restore,
Then he would be the kind of man
you know "I think he should"
Yes he would be more loving, sweet-
more gentle, kind, and good,

Chorus

So Lord please help the other man—I know he's not like me,
'Cause Lord you know I'm always
kind and sweet as I can be,
And Lord I'm always trying to lend a helping hand,

So Lord won't you please talk to him,
and help him understand,

But the Lord Said,

My child I've listened to you, and I know your mortal frame,
And I love you and I sure am glad
when you call upon my name,
But if you ever want to see that brother change his way,
Just change your life to fit the one, you prayed for him today.

Dusty and Jann

Dusty and Jann live up the street,
In a little house that is very neat.
If you go there you'll agree with this poet,
That they are great hosts and all should know it.

Jann will greet you with a smile,
That will make your visit very worthwhile,
And Dusty supplies a little wit,
That will catch you off guard 'til you're used to it.

Kody will bark and sound real tough,
But he'll settle down soon enough,
And quietly rest in a living room chair,
So you'd hardly notice that he is there.

So come—sit down, relax a while,
And share a thought, a snack, a smile,
You'll find it hard to leave, but then,
You're always welcome back again.

C. R. Lord
8/12/2004 at 2:00 p.m.
Dedicated to my Sis, and her Husband

Non-Poetic Writings

Introduction

Non-Poetic writings consist of a few articles covering a variety of topics. There are articles that the Lord gave me to write, and a couple with a little humor. As with everything in this book, my foremost aim is to honor and glorify God and bless, exhort, comfort, and otherwise touch the lives of my readers in a way that will bring positive results and draw them closer to God. I believe with all my heart that there is no higher calling than to know God intimately, seek to learn what He would have us do, and obey Him implicitly and without question! The intimacy will insure that we know whose voice we hear and make obeying considerably easier to the willing heart and more disconcerting to those who hear Him but fear what He may ask of them. Remember, He will not test us above what we are able to bear.

It has been a source of much concern for me that in this generation the church has become non-offensive and entirely too careful about what it presents to the world. We have failed miserably in bringing the conviction that results in conversion experiences that produce lives deeply consecrated to God. Some of what is written in the non-poetic pages will express that concern in a way that may cause some of my readers to deem it uncharitable or as coming from a self-righteous heart. Rest assured that I know my shortcomings, and much of what I have written is true in my life as well as the lives of many of God's people across the world.

If these writings provoke others to serious self-examination, as is recommended in the scripture, that brings repentance and power to live as Christ has called us to live, then I will gladly be criticized, justly or unjustly, by those who are offended by my writing for whatever reason. A not too often quoted verse is the ground I stand on in this matter, and it is found in Galatians 1:10 which reads, "For do I now persuade men, or God? or do I seek to please men? for if I yet pleased men, I should not be the servant of Christ."

Our main purpose in this life should be to please God, not men! I am firmly convinced that to live to please God above all else will never bring us the approval of the masses either in or out of the body of Christ. With that in mind I present these gifts, without apology, to the reader. May God be glorified in what is accomplished is my greatest hope and deepest desire!

A Day Without Doors

March 1985

I woke up at 7:00 a.m. and was astonished to find that the doorways in my bedroom had vanished. Somewhat fearful and trembling, I dressed and climbed out the side window of our house. I ran to the front porch and looked up only to find the door was missing there as well. In stunned surprise, I hurried to the back of the house and found the back door and cellar entrances both gone. As I was about to panic I remembered that I still had windows, but my momentary relief collapsed when I realized I had locked them to discourage break-ins during the night. I thought to myself, "If I deal with this now, I'll be late for work." I hurriedly closed the bedroom window I'd come out of, and started down the street.

Suddenly, I began to notice something very strange. All the doors were gone from all the houses. People who were up at this early hour were scrambling in and out of windows and around their houses and garages in frantic amazement. Even the doors on the cars and trucks were gone, and the clamor being raised all around was waking the entire neighborhood.

Now, I began to really worry as I walked on in a fog of unbelief. "This can't be happening!" I thought as I stared incredulously, this must be some colossal hoax!"

Arriving at work, I found others already there in a frenzy of excited chatter. The doors leading into the factory were gone. Outside every home and business people gathered in terror. There were no doors to be seen anywhere. I began to run to friends and relatives' homes, city hall, the drug store, and the bank. Everywhere people were facing the same dilemma, as something near to insanity prevailed throughout the city. What could have happened!? What could be done!?

Finally, I reached the church I was attending, and found the Pastor outside in an agitated state much like everyone else. I felt myself on the verge of hopelessness. The weight of this problem came crashing in on me, and I began to scream.

Suddenly, I woke up in a cold sweat in my room, and in deep relief and gratitude

I realized it was all a dream.

In the morning stillness, I thought of the millions who were anxiously seeking a door of escape from the fears and uncertainties of life—a door, which would assure them of comfort and peace, in a world, filled with treachery and unrest.

Then I remembered the words of Jesus; "*I am the door.*" *John 10:9*

C. R. Lord

A Word To Those Who Call Themselves Christians

It is a great tragedy that millions today are blinded by sin, and the devil rules them without their knowledge. Sadly many are children. In part, the fault lies at the door of the church in every generation that has failed to obey the Lord. The following poem is a wake up call to us!

Hear O' Church

Oh the wondrous love of Jesus when He came to save,
Oh the mystery of His glorious victory o'er the grave,
Oh the awesome weight we carry that would do His will,
Oh the sinful hearts who hear Him and reject Him still,

As we hear His awful warning to a sinful race,
Can we sleep while men are dying at an awful pace?
Can we rest while souls are feeding on the husks of life?
Can we see the millions lost and stay back from the strife?

Now the Master sends a call to those who bear His name,
Will we listen and obey, or hang our heads in shame?
When the roll is called up yonder, will we meet someone,
Who, through our response to Him
has come to know God's Son?

Brethren let us rise above the little things that keep,
Us from running to the battle for the Lord's lost sheep,
Let's go on, nor fear of dying, keep us from the strife,
Snatching many from hell's fires to eternal life.

> Let us fight, with banners flying, every evil foe,
> Shouting victory, striking boldly, never letting go,
> Striking out with strong assurance in that Blessed One,
> Who will bring us to the kingdom
> with a sweet "Well Done."
>
> Was a higher call e'er given? I must answer No!
> Do we wish to fail Him now, who has loved us so?
> Oh eternal, matchless glory; How can we delay?
> Let us give our all for Jesus! Let's begin today!
>
> *C. R. Lord*

I just finished watching a video showing the terrible calamities that fall upon the earth from time to time in the form of earthquakes, floods, avalanches, typhoons, hurricanes, raging fires, tornadoes and more. It seemed to me as I watched the horror and devastation that the film was overlooking one very important consideration. Hundreds of thousands of people were dying all over the world through these tragedies, and yet, the larger tragedy of those who went out into eternity lost and without hope never entered the picture or the mind of the videos creator.

I am not surprised that the secular media that created the program missed this most important fact, but I am appalled that those of us who call ourselves Christians would probably view this video and be totally oblivious to the very same thing. The body of Christ in this generation has become stagnant, fat, lazy and comfortable in a generation that very desperately needs to hear the gospel of Jesus Christ presented to them in the power and anointing of the Holy Spirit. I would not be surprised to hear the words uncharitable, self-righteous, and like epithets hurled at me in the writing of these words, but were I to seek to please man then I would no longer be the servant of Christ. (Galatians 1:10)

Certainly such an accusation as I bring must be substantiated before it can be given any credibility, but in order for it to be substantiated, it must be at least objectively examined in the light of current events or the lack thereof. I do not see this as an insurmountable task given the current state of world affairs; especially, in the country which some call the Land of the Free and the Home of the Brave. The following are points of interest to me that I feel substantiate my accusations, and I offer them without apology for those who are still open to the truth:

Through the Internet, Christians worldwide have access to multiple resources for promoting the gospel. We have web sites that reach to every corner of the world. In the more affluent countries, and even in some of the less affluent, we have access to more books, tapes, videos, CD Roms, gospel tracts, brochures, churches, radios, television shows, and a host more tools than I care to name here. With all this, the conversion rate that is reported by all the organizations on earth is a paltry sum by comparison to the accessibility of the gospel.

The gospel presented by the vast bulk of churches today is hardly the gospel that the apostles and prophets preached prior to and since the advent of Christ. We are sorely lacking the one thing that alters the destinies of men and turns them to the one source of salvation. Acts 1:8 "But ye shall receive POWER, after that the Holy Ghost is come upon you!" The lack of power is clearly evident in the church where so few are converted to the gospel, and of those converted so few are taught that commitment is a normal way of life for those who truly want to serve Christ. Millions of Christians have become so entangled with the world that it takes a very close examination to find out who is who! We are not the off scouring of the world, or strangers and pilgrims, or peculiar people and we certainly are not hated as "He" was.

Atheists, agnostics, Witches, and a host of other ungodly among us are continually touted and sanctioned as ok with men and women around the world. Pornography floods the world through the internet and every other resource, we are killing our own children through abortion, non-Christian groups are being recognized as Christian and their deviant practices are attributed to true Christianity further alienating the general public from the gospel of Jesus Christ. Teen crime rates increase, sex crimes have become bolder and, in some cases, protected with absurd excuses or encouraged as what should have been the norm all through the years if only rigid fundamentalism hadn't interfered with sexual freedom. The Bible is deemed to be the old fashioned standard of rigid extremists or totally irrelevant to this generation. Liberalism parades it unholy wares on every front seducing young and old alike. We are surrounded by humanism, new age ideology, cults and every bird of prey, open mockery of God and Jesus Christ appear on every side, sexual freedom and recreation are theme songs everywhere, and yet the church seems powerless against this floodtide of filth and degradation and international calamity.

Read the words of an eminent minister (circa 1895),

No Christian man can open his eyes and not see that

a new class has sprung up, such as Christendom has never before seen; highly cultured men who explore the heights and depth of the Universe seeking knowledge of its laws and forces, but who acknowledge no Divine will or purpose, contemptuous of theology, without object of worship, confident in the boundless development of science, and boastful of the glorious future of humanity." If we were not so blind in this generation we would see that the condition that this godly man saw has only increased in this generation to the point of saturating our world with its foolish ideologies, while we who call ourselves Christian have done little to stem the tide.

This same man wrote the following:

> The press cannot create the spirit of an age, it can only give it utterance. Its power lies in its ability to give publicity to principles and movements, or to withhold it. According to its position may proclaim or may ignore vital truths and facts; may give prominence to events and men or pass them by in silence. We may note also, the periodical press regards all subjects as coming within its sphere sacred and secular, everything which affects humanity. Nothing is too high or too low. It sits in judgment upon all men, upon all questions; and its judgments are often uttered in a very dogmatic way as irreversible." Those who are willing to objectively examine the content of today's magazines and newspapers, radio and television press releases and etc. will find this man to have

vision clearly in touch with the corrupted press of this age.

Where does all this take us? How can we reverse this horrible trend to mediocrity while the world runs headlong on its course to Hell and eternal damnation? While the hope lies in Gods Word it is only a hope unless the words are burned upon our hearts through a personal and corporate repentance toward God and a complete submission to His working in and through us for the good of all.

Here is the key. It is our individual responsibility to respond to God in His way to see the results we long for if we truly love Him!

If my people who are called by my name will humble themselves and pray, and turn from their wicked ways, then will I hear from Heaven and THEN will I heal their land. The power we need will come when we repent and seek the Lord with all our hearts; when we are willing to sacrifice all for Him and those he died for; 'then and only then!'

It is amazing to me how we gather week after week and spend time in the house of God professing love for Him, singing the songs of Zion, praising Him and by all outward appearances serving Him and being faithful to Him. Yet we are blinded to the fact that God gave us two commands 'Thou shalt love the Lord your God with all your heart and all your soul and all your mind and all your strength and thou shalt love thy neighbor as thyself.'

Am I to believe that we love our neighbor, and yet never speak a word to them that would deliver them from whatever has blinded them to their impending danger if they die without Christ? Am I to believe that we love God when the word of God declares without apology "If you see your brother in need and have the means to meet his need and you don't how can the love of Christ dwell in you?" A man once led his entire community to Christ after much weeping and prayer, and he wrote that if his blood were ink he would not spare one drop if it would rescue one person from being eternally separated from God.

Where is our compassion? Where is our reflection of the heart of God that yearns over the lost and dying sinner? The world is aching to hear from someone who has heard from God and will bring forth the Word without compromise in love or in wrath according to the need. It is this author's belief that because of the spiritual deadness of many among us in the older generations God is raising up an army of young men and women under our noses that will bring an awakening to the church and to the nations of the world. I wonder; will we continue to sleep or will we take up this burden and seek God until He pours out revival in this sin-laden nation and the world around us? When we finally stand before Him and the whole world passes by the judgment seat of Christ, will we hear … "Well done thou good and faithful servant" or "Why call ye me Lord, Lord and do not the things that I say?" Where do you stand?

The year 2008 is upon us. Will we continue on in our

spiritual deadness or awake to the multitudes that are dying all around us and passing into a Christless eternity?

C. R. Lord

Child Of Darkness Or Light?

It is amazing that so many people living today and through past ages will avoid what is the most important to them. Just a few examples will clarify what is easily identifiable to us all.

1. We know that we should eat properly and exercise regularly but most of us stuff ourselves on foods that make us obese or at least harm us physically, creating poor health as the years progress and exercise little or not at all.

2. We know that the persons most qualified to take care of us when we are sick are trained medical professionals but we often wait until we are in serious need before consulting with them. We could have prevented a lot of needless suffering but we disregarded what we knew to be the best course of action.

3. We take our first cigarette or beer or joint, and the acrid taste of smoke and the bitter taste of beer warn us to avoid these things because they create numerous physical problems, and psychological problems, and yet we continue in them to the point of physical and psychological deterioration.

4. Our conscience tells us that what we are doing to ourselves or others is morally wrong, but we run past the warning signs because we believe what we want will make us feel good or fit in with a group or whatever excuse we use to justify our actions.

5. We know that we should prepare for death because

we have heard the stories of poor estate handling and the abuses to other survivors of family loss but we never get a will done or set aside money for all the expenses tied to funerals and burials and unsettled debts.

There is one thing that we all must prepare for that is far greater in importance than all these things above, and yet multitudes of people never consider it or put it off. They live as if they would live forever on earth and can make this decision at some time in the future. We go on in foolish ignorance somehow deluded into thinking that we have control over our lives and all the while we are clothed in darkness that clouds our vision to what really matters and we find ourselves facing death much sooner than we imagined, and we are unprepared.

You alone can answer this question: Are you a child of darkness or a child of light? What do you base your answer on? Are you sure beyond all doubt that your answer is correct? What if it isn't—how can you change? Who would you go to in order to find real truth? Is your answer real to you but offering you a false peace?

Imagine living an entire lifetime in deception and waking up in eternity only to find out that what you believed all your life was a lie! Whether you want to face up to it or not, you must find out before you die because there is life beyond the grave! You have an immortal soul, and God will bring you into judgment after you leave this life.

And as it is appointed unto men once to die—but—after this the judgment.

(Hebrews 9:27 KJV)

I ask you again, are you a child of darkness or a child of light? If you choose to ignore this one thing it will prove to be a greater error than all those mentioned above put together. To go out into eternity unprepared is foolish considering the great pains God went through to prevent it.

> For God so loved the world, that He gave His only begotten Son, that whosoever believeth in Him, should not perish but have everlasting life.
>
> (John 3:16 KJV)

The greatest preparation you can make in life is to trust in the one person who cared enough to die a cruel and brutal death for you and can deliver you from eternal punishment for your sins. He endured scourging and mockery and spitting and even entered the realm of Hell to suffer for you—*the just for the unjust*—that He could deliver you from walking in darkness and eternal death and total separation from God forever. Coming to Him is simple - so simple that a child can do it. Confess that you are a sinner and that you are truly sorry for your sin. Ask Him to forgive you and cleanse you of your sin fully and completely. Then pray that He will lead and guide you for the rest of your life. Surrender totally to His leadership - He paid the price for you and deserves your loyalty. His name is Jesus and He is waiting to hear from you. Won't you make this extremely important decision today before it is eternally too late?

C. R. Lord

I Find Myself Laughing

It is early in the morning, 12:45 a.m. on July 13, 2004, and I am alone with my thoughts.

It is wonderfully quiet here with my wife and all the children in bed or away from home.

I find myself laughing at what I have been thinking because it seems to have depth and yet it is about our lack of depth—a strange paradox! I have been thinking about our learned and wise men in this nation and around the world, and how much we have been able to accomplish during the short span of life that this earth has existed. My thoughts have turned to all our academic prowess and our self assured wisdom (or is it wisdumb?) and how we parade ourselves and others around as educated and sophisticated scholars. It is at this point that I cannot help but laugh!

From academia my mind drifts to all our marvelous inventions and our technical advances throughout the years, and how rapidly we are advancing in that area and once again I find myself laughing!

You see - we are finite creatures and extremely limited in intelligence, creativity, and all the other things that we hold as marks of achievement. It has been estimated that the most intelligent men ever to live on this planet use only one tenth of one percent of their brain. *One tenth of one percent!* This is a ludicrous figure. Imagine what could be achieved if we were able to harness 10% or 20% or 50% or more. We are barely touching the surface of our capabilities and yet we swagger and boast as though we had actually achieved great things! The picture makes me chuckle to myself and in the back of my mind I can see how ridiculous we must look to God. As a matter of fact, the Bible says that "the foolishness of God is wiser than the wisdom of man." It further states that "Every man at his very best is altogether vanity."

Consider God now in comparison. God is infinite! Infinity has no beginning or end. It is without measure. It is incomprehensible. It is plainly out of our reach. To illustrate God's superiority over man consider that God has such vast wisdom that He knows every thought and act ever thought or done from before time began on earth and beyond into the vast ages of eternity. There is not one particle or iota of knowledge that has ever gotten past Him - nor will there ever be! In the words of one writer, "God knows everything past, present and future instantly and without any effort." God doesn't ever have to guess about anything, He is never surprised about anything and is never alarmed about anything. In addition, there is nothing that He could ever learn because he already possesses knowledge of everything. He knows us from the very first spark of life in the fertilization of an egg to the very last breath we draw, and He knows this in intricate detail in the life of every person who is alive, has ever lived and will live in the future, and He knows it better than anyone else. There is never any knowledge that can enter into God from outside of Him because He is the center of all knowledge in the universe. How tragically we pale in comparison to Him!

Is it any wonder then that this world is in such a mess? Men have somehow begun to think that God is a relic of the past and has no bearing on their future. These men are heralded as great scholars and thinkers in our time by multitudes of misinformed, uneducated and unspiritual people. Even among those who deem themselves to be spiritual our concepts of God are tragically shallow or completely vague in comparison to whom He really is! He is more than good all the time or colossal, more than mighty and strong, matchless beyond our wildest dreams and imaginings, He is perfect in all His ways; perfect knowledge and wisdom, perfect compassion, perfectly just in all His decisions, and perfect love. *'All the adjectives existing in all the languages of the world arranged in their very best sequence would fall far short of describing one single thing about God adequately.'* If I were to continue this thought to its conclusion it would never reach a conclusion because all that could ever be written about God would, at last, have to be inconclusive!

Excuse me while I laugh again! God is so wonderful and awesome and phenomenal and—Oh, what's the use? I give up! One thing that I know for sure about Him is that He has loved me out of my sin and ignorance and into His wonderful family through His Son Jesus Christ! "I once was blind, but now I see." Amazing grace! Our God is an awesome God!

Don't worry if your intellect can't comprehend God. Your heart will once you come to know Him, and as you go deeper with Him—you will laugh with me.

C. R. Lord

The Secular Media and Christianity

I would be amused, if it weren't so distasteful, at the total lack of understanding demonstrated by the secular media concerning Christians and what they believe concerning various issues. It is akin to aliens coming from space, looking over our society and explaining it from their other worldly point of view. The absurdity of it all would be plain to anyone who lives on this planet.

I believe the reason for this is that the media think everyone who wears the title Protestant or Catholic or a host of other groups is Christian without the most important qualification that they become part of the family of God. Tragically, some even think that the entire human race is part of God's family which is a grave error. The Bible clearly delineates between children of light and children of darkness—the only two spiritual families in the universe.

Becoming a child of God involves repentance for our sinful ways, acceptance of Christ as Savior and Lord and a lifetime of loving and serving God and dealing with the sin nature that lives within all of us. Of course, many believe that there are many ways to God, however Jesus eliminated that possibility by proclaiming Himself as the only way—John 14:6 clearly states, "Jesus said unto him, I am the way, the truth, and the life, no man comes unto the Father but by me." Further, it is stated in Acts 4:12, "Neither is there salvation in any other; for there is no other name under heaven given among men whereby we must be saved." When a person accepts this in their hearts and allows God to do the deep cleansing work that adoption into His family involves they are given the gift of the Holy Spirit to teach and guide them in the things of

God. This is where the separation comes between darkness (false spiritual understanding, knowledge and wisdumb) and light (true spiritual understanding, knowledge and wisdom). Apart from the leading and guidance of the Holy Spirit there is no real understanding of truth.

For the secular media to attempt to understand Christianity apart from this conversion experience is ludicrous, and much that is written in the press bears this out.

Christian convictions based upon the Word of God are smeared openly and we are accused of being hate-mongers, homophobic, and whatever the press deems to be appropriate, including anti-abortionist instead of pro-life (a subtle form of word twisting called semantics).

The press confuses our stance because they do not understand that our real concern is not the issues themselves but the eternal destiny of those who continue to pursue what the Bible calls sin. They do not understand that God's love working through His people will always stand against that which will destroy individuals and the nation they live in for the sake of those who do not understand God's mercy toward a wicked and perverse generation. In a world that has gone mad with liberalism, Christians must of necessity fulfill Christ's words, "If they hated me, they will hate you also because as I am not of this world neither are you."

Before writing off this letter as uncharitable, understand that this writer followed the ways of the world for many years before coming to a saving knowledge of Christ. I am very familiar with the spirit that rules those who have not come to a saving knowledge of Christ, and certainly grieve over those of you who will read this and reject it because you would rather follow your opinion than accept the truth that is presented here. Spiritual darkness is the worst sickness on this planet—all other evils come from it, and the only solution to it is deliverance through Jesus Christ.

It is my earnest hope that some who read this letter from my heart will trust Him to deliver them and guide them through this life and throughout eternity.

C. R. Lord

Reflections On Important Matters

I guess a good jumping off point would be to clearly define what constitutes matters that are important to life. There is a broad scope of things that are considered important in life according to the world view held by the individual concerned. There are, however, only two perspectives on every issue that concerns mankind and I will base my analysis on those two views.

The first view, I would like to examine is the worldly view or as the Bible calls it the carnal nature. The carnal nature is that part of all men and women and children that cares nothing for anything that is spiritual in nature unless the spiritual can be molded and shaped to please the carnal nature within that person. The focus of this part of our being is on those things which will bring the most comfort and pleasure to us and in virtually every case is selfish in nature.

The carnal nature loves religion that has no absolutes and no dogma to force it to examine itself seriously in the light of eternity. It dotes on the sweets of religion and hates passionately the negative side of deity - especially the judgments of God. It considers all who insist on moral standards as deviants and misfits who want to "push" their beliefs on everyone. Strangely enough, when in excruciating pain or deep problems that seem unsolvable these people cry out to the God that they would otherwise have nothing to do with. After God bails them out of the situation they created they once again go about their merry way forgetting Him and cursing those who love Him.

The carnal nature spends itself on material possessions, luxury, any and every form of relaxation and recreation, sexual lust, excessive consumption of alcohol and/or drugs, movies, secular music, parties, religion that is comfortable and provides a showcase for their "piety," computer games and other expensive toys that waste precious time that could be used more constructively, and everything that destroys any hope of preparing for eternal life - which, by the way, most of, if not all of these people think they can ignore or at least put off for a later date.

The second view is totally spiritual in nature, and believes that "living in the flesh" is an abomination to God. These individuals have strong convictions that this life is not all there is, and that there is life beyond the grave. They also believe that there are moral absolutes handed down to all mankind by a Holy and Omnipotent God who will hold all people accountable for their obedience to or rejection of His written and spoken commandments. These people believe themselves to be totally unworthy of God's forgiveness, and rightly so. They believe that even though they are unworthy God has forgiven them anyway through His Son Jesus Christ and saved them from eternal life in a place of eternal punishment and suffering—a place many people are telling one another to go to and don't believe in. Hell is not a popular subject in the church or out of it, and it is rarely spoken of in the soft preaching of this generation, but those who are truly spiritual-minded have a strong belief in its existence. Somehow these people think it is important enough to warn people not to go there, and their concern earns them the hatred of the very people they are trying to save while these same people readily applaud those who are paving the way for them to go there. The devil, who many also believe is a little creature in a red suit with horns and a pitchfork, is laughing in his sleeve at their ignorance.

But of course it is nothing to worry about because those who reject God and His Son Jesus Christ and the outdated and antiquated teachings of the Bible which are not relevant to this generation certainly know for a fact that the devil isn't real either.

The spiritual person seems to be more concerned with the eternal things and not the material and carnal because they believe that the Bible teaches them, "Love not the world, neither the things that are in the world; and set your affections on things above and not on the things of the earth, for you are dead and your life is hid with Christ in God." This person honestly believes that the Bible is relevant, not only in this world but also in the world to come. They somehow find it believable that God answers prayer, and have actually prayed and gotten answers—some of them very precise and specific. As a matter of fact, many of the answers were personalized so that there was no way that it would fit any other circumstance. They believe that studying the Bible will help them with any circumstance in life, and that trusting in the author of the Bible will actually help them face death with confidence. They also believe that on the other side of the grave they will have joy and peace with God, angels and fellow believers forever.

Possessions and money and relaxation and recreation and all the other earthly comforts and pleasures seem to have little allure for these individuals, and they hold them as useful but temporal. They do not spend their lives to gain prestige and honor from men, because they would much rather have praise from God. Somehow they seem to enjoy blessing others more than they care about being blessed. They find their children to be a joy and blessing and not a burden. They are the total opposite of their carnal counterpart, and they fulfill the Word of God which declares, "You are the righteousness of God in Christ Jesus." Imagine! A sinner justified and exalted to such prominence! And without taking on airs of self-righteousness because they keenly feel their own unworthiness.

The Bible says: *"Straight is the gate and narrow is the way that leads to eternal life and few there be that find it, but broad is the road to destruction and multitudes go in that direction."*

Are you spiritual or carnal? Can you walk with God alone if necessary or are you a crowd pleaser? Do you reject God and moral absolutes?

Where will you spend eternity? Before you put another purchase on your credit card, before you hit the weights, before you step into that sauna, before you walk out onto that field, before you cook the next meal, or do any of the multitudes of other things that fill your life, you better know the answer to these questions, not only in your head, but in your heart. To continue to ignore these vital issues is like holding a lighted stick of dynamite to see how far down the fuse will burn before it blows you up or you put it out. None of us knows how long we will live. Today may be the first day of the rest of your life... in eternity!

C. R. Lord

Leadership

Leadership must be gauged by the life of Christ alone. Perfection isn't alterable. Observe the following points concerning His leadership.

- L oyalty, a major factor in leadership, was exemplified in Him who said, "My meat is to do the will of Him who sent me." Our heart's cry must be, "Thy Will be done!"

- E ndurance was projected by Him who endured mockery and humiliation among many evils, including the cross. We must endure through these also.

- A uthority was His, and men knew that "He spoke as one having authority." No one desires to follow a man who fails to exercise authority.

- D etermination was evidenced when "He set His face to go to Jerusalem." We must establish goals and exercise unrelenting persistence in accomplishing them.

- E xample was perfected in Christ who Himself said, "I do always those things which please the Father." No honest man could condemn this example.

- R eliability was personified in the Savior's word and in every facet of His life. None were turned away who came to Him in need. God help us!

- S ubmission in the life of Jesus is unparalleled for "He as a sheep before His shearers was dumb. This is the hardest of lessons for proud man.

- H oliness found its truest meaning in "The Lamb without spot or blemish." Being constantly under the spotlight demands that we live pure lives.

- I nitiative began when "He took upon Himself the form of a man." He was willing to take the first step. We must initiate action as we lead.

- P rayer was our Lord's lifestyle. Communion with the Father was His Supreme delight! Without this most important factor all else is worthless.

All of these must be prefaced with love!

C. R. Lord

Management

May 5, 1980

Management equals responsibility and accountability. Many qualities are essential to good management. A few are listed below. Managers should be:

M anagement oriented, without which they must become overwhelmed and frustrated causing a complete breakdown in subordinates and work as well.

A ltruistic, for ministry and service to others is the official capacity of those who would lead. Personal needs, unfulfilled, spell disaster.

N arrow-minded, because the goals and objectives must be met. To turn aside for any lesser need would be foolish. God has called us to victory.

A ttentive to the events occurring on every side. All transactions or incidents affecting one person affect everyone, and eventually the entire organization.

G lorifying God, for this alone is the primary purpose for all existence. Apart from this, all else is only vain effort and offensive to God.

E xplicit in every communication whether written or verbal. Failure here has caused the loss of much time, money, material and manpower.

M odern, by using all available media to capitalize on information and keep abreast or ahead of the times and circumstances and benefit everyone.

E nthusiastic about their program and their people. When subordinates see this, they get excited too, and when superiors see this, they promote you.

N eat in appearance, work and home life. An orderly home is generally a sign of an orderly life. Our God is a God of order and we should reflect Him.

T eachable, because no man, regardless of his background, has all of the knowledge on any subject at any time. God alone is Omniscient!

Management—Impossible, except in Christ!

C. R. Lord

The Man Who Would Please Everyone

On page 148 is a picture of the man who would please everyone—I got the idea long ago, but instead of drawing the picture myself, I searched far and wide for someone else to do it. After years of frustration I figured that the Lord planted the idea in my head so He must have wanted me to do it, and so I did.

Please notice this man. Personally, I believe it would be hard not to if he were walking the streets today even with all the bizarre fashions and hairstyles that we see paraded around as if they were normal or to be desired by the masses.

The first thing about him is that his face is half-man and half-woman, and he has a variety of hair styles or hairless styles or in between. This will please women, and men who love long hair on themselves and women. It will also please punk rockers and balding men. His face only has half a beard so as not to offend the clean-shaven or those who love to grow beards and think themselves distinguished. He only has half a pair of glasses which will please those with failing sight and good sight. He has an earring in one ear and a cigarette in his mouth underneath a half mustache. These hardly need explained.

The symbol, which many call the "peace symbol," above his pocket is a satanic symbol in reality designating the cross of Jesus Christ turned upside down and broken which is an attempt to mock Christ's sacrifice. Never fear though, because our intrepid fellow also has "King Jesus" on his backpack to soothe Christians.

The top part of his clothing is a mixture of military and collegiate design and his upper body sports a wimpy arm for the geeks and a muscular arm for the jocks. Of course, Mom has to get in there somewhere so he has her tattooed on.

Around his waist is a belt and a sash which hold up his amazing pants, which are pleated and clean cut on the one side and patchwork with holes on the other. The businessmen will love one and the hippies of the 70's or the young people of the new generation will love the other. To complete the façade our hero even has a wooden peg leg in order to appear non-offensive to the disabled.

A final note of interest is that he is a magna cum laude graduate of PPU and he proudly displays the letters on his college attire. PPU, by the way stands for People Pleasers University.

Now that we can see how absurd it would be to try and please everyone it should wake us up to the reality that we need to be who we really are inside. The Bible tells me that, "God does not see as man sees; for man looks on the outward appearance but God looks on the heart." Nobody can please everybody, but everyone should want to please God—after all, He is the one who gave us life in the first place.

© 2001 C.R. Lord

Baby Congratulations

Welcome to that wonderful *adult education class*—parenthood! This class has no special hours as it is conducted morning, noon, and night.

The *teacher* is often very demanding, and even requires the students to attend classes on weekends, very late at night and very early in the morning. Don't worry though—you'll just have a *bawl*!

You'll have plenty of *home*work, but little, if any time to study and prepare for the tests! You will experience many *changes*, but the results will be well worth it!

As you grow and mature, the *teacher* will be less demanding, and may even let you teach the class.

Of course, graduation is the best part—when you finally get to go out on your own!

>Originated August 2, 1985
>For Ed and Doris Watts
>On the birth of their daughter
>Faith Rebecca

Rick's Pawn Shop

Come to Rick's *pawn* shop where the customer is always *king*, and you are guaranteed that you'll never be *rooked*!

The shop is endorsed by *Bishop* Cantrell who had a set made here for *Queen* Annabelle. We are open only at *knight* from 5:00 to 9:30 p.m. Why not bring your *mate* and take our product home to your *castle?* We guarantee that you will never get *board* while using our fine sets.

Chess in case you were wondering; we accept money orders, cash, or *check* in payment for our fine sets.

Thank you,

The Management

Some Closing Thoughts

I have walked this planet for sixty-four years as of September 27, 2006. I have seen many people come and go and many events come and go which, in and of itself would make a compelling book. I have had thoughts of writing a life story many times, however it has never materialized.

This collection of ideas and poetry springs from a dramatic change in my life when Jesus Christ reached out to me in 1974 and transformed my entire life. Prior to that my life was a mess.

I started drinking while serving in the United States Air Force and was absolutely ripped drunk many times. From alcohol, I turned to drugs, and eventually became a drug dealer on the streets of my hometown. Everything you read about that lifestyle I experienced in some measure. Some things I experienced by observing others but much of it I experienced first hand. At one point, I became so disenchanted with life that I decided to kill myself. I am so deeply grateful to God that I didn't succeed.

The first time I woke up to reality was when I was arrested and put into Broward County Prison in Ft. Lauderdale, Florida. I was given a misdemeanor charge when I could have faced up to fifteen years. During my incarceration, I took time to review my life and I discovered that I had no future and had never planned one. I had no clear cut purpose for living except to please myself and work as little as possible so I could spend my time partying. I knew that I had tried everything I had any desire to try and none of it satisfied me. The only place I had not turned was to God, so I began my search to find out if He was real in jail.

To make a long story short, God revealed Himself to me in such a way that there was no possibility of doubt, and I have been walking with Him and He with me for over thirty-two years. I have experienced much in the course of that time but it is all vastly superior to my previous life, and I can say that of everything whether it is positive or negative. God has a habit of turning everything into something good for those who love Him. It is a wonderful way to live!

The poetry comes from my heart, and some of it comes from my own personal experience. "My Surrender" speaks of my attempted surrender and God's mercy. "Wee Little Hands" comes from my experience raising our seven children. "Hear O' Church" comes from a burden God has put upon me to see the body of Christ walk in victory as God intended that we should. "I Set My Face" is a story of failure in ministry that I went through in Indianapolis, Indiana and then later in Louisville, Kentucky. "Leadership and Management" are final exams from Bible College.

I have no animosity toward anyone. I say this because some may interpret my writings and the "Man Who Would Please Everyone" as an attack rather than a concerned statement. There is enough grief in this world without me adding to it.

My purpose in this writing is only that the reader may find something to challenge or lift them or stir them on to greater heights. My absolute first priority is that God may be exalted and honored and glorified for He alone deserves our very best in all we do and say and think! I pray earnestly that those who read this collection of thoughts will be richly blessed in the way that is most needed in their lives and that they may draw something from them that they can use to bless others as well.

I can seriously and truthfully say that I love you unconditionally no matter who you are or what your life is like because the love I have to share is not mine, but placed there by a wonderful, holy God, who is love and who proved His love by sacrificing His "only" Son for each of us.

Oh, that all men would come to know and love Him! There is no true peace without Him who alone loves you more than you love yourself and more than anyone ever could love you.

My prayer for everyone on earth is found in Ephesians 3:14–19. I can't conceive that there could be more blessing contained in any literature in the entire world than what is contained in these few verses. May God make them a reality in your life and mine.

C. R. Lord